PSI SUCCESSFUL BUSINESS LIBRARY

Retail in Detail

How to Start and Manage a Small Retail Business

Ronald L. Bond

Linda Pinkham, Editor

The Oasis Press® / PSI Research
Grants Pass, Oregon
091896

Published by The Oasis Press®
© 1996 by Ronald L. Bond

This publication is designed to provide accurate and authoritative information in regard to the subject matter covered. It is sold with the understanding that the publisher is not engaged in rendering legal, accounting, or other professional service. If legal advice or other expert assistance is required, the services of a competent professional person should be sought.
> *— from a declaration of principles jointly adopted by a committee of the American Bar Association and a committee of publishers.*

Managing Editor: Linda Pinkham
Assistant Editors: Vickie Reierson and Camille Akin
Book Designer: Constance C. Dickinson
Typographer: Jan Olsson
Cover Designers: Steven Burns and C. C. Dickinson, based on a design by Mark Kleinfeld Design, Inc.

Please direct any comments, questions, or suggestions regarding this book to The Oasis Press®/PSI Research:

> Editorial Department
> 300 North Valley Drive
> Grants Pass, OR 97526
> (541) 479-9464

The Oasis Press® is a Registered Trademark of Publishing Services, Inc., an Oregon corporation doing business as PSI Research.

Library of Congress Cataloging-in-Publication Data
Bond, Ronald L., 1939–
    Retail in detail : how to start and manage a small retail business
  / Ronald L. Bond ; Linda Pinkham, editor.
    p. ; cm.
    Includes index.
    ISBN 1-55571-371-8 (pbk. : alk. paper)
    1. Retail trade. 2. Small business. I. Title.
  HF5429.86116 1996
  658.8'7--dc20   96-1648

Printed in the United States of America
First edition 10 9 8 7 6 5 4 3 2 1 0   Revision Code: 96AA

 Printed on recycled paper when available.

Table
of Contents

Part III – Retail Business Management

Part IV – The Appendices

Preface

Writing a book was about the farthest thing from my mind when, in 1985, my wife and I decided to open our own retail store. This book shares with you what we learned and our experience of starting our retail gift shop, Homespun Cottage.

My wife Susie always had a talent for decorating, while I had skills in management. Our objective was to achieve a lifelong ambition to combine these talents for decorating, crafts, business, and management experience into a tangible enterprise that would also, hopefully, produce some extra income and provide a nest egg for retirement. Of course, we also harbored that secret dream of all entrepreneurs that our shop would prove wildly successful, be franchised nationwide, and make us millionaires by age fifty. Okay, so we got started a little late to fulfill our Horatio Alger fantasy by thirty-something, but better late than never!

Now, after more than ten years in business, we have yet to see our store name in lights in shopping centers across the nation, but we do have two stores across town from each other, which is a start. And we have achieved some financial success and have developed a business that is debt free and worth enough to give us some additional financial security in our golden years, whatever those are. We have also gained a great amount of experience, met many new and wonderful people — along with a few grouches — broadened our range of interests, and strengthened our relationships with each other and with the rest of our family. So we consider the venture a success, even though we are not rich and famous, yet.

Our family situation when we began our business was such that Susie could devote full-time to the shop, and I would be able to assist on a daily basis, while maintaining full-time outside employment. We had two sons, one working part-time and attending the local community college, and the other in high school. At that point, we reasoned the time was propitious for our venture into the world of business since our children were fairly independent.

I use vacation time to help during buying trips and at other times of peak need. The buying trips have proven to be what the Cajun people call *lagniappe*, meaning something special and extra that is not expected. We have had many wonderful trips together all over the United States.

Neither of us had any real experience as retailers when we began, but we believed we had the basic ingredients for a successful store if we planned carefully, were fiscally prudent, and executed our plans carefully and deliberately.

We started serious planning for our first store in the spring of 1985, opened the store in September, and operated it successfully through a period of changing economic climate. Then, in spring 1991, we began planning for our second store, which we opened in August of 1991, in a shopping center across town from the first. Through this experience, which can best be characterized as trial and error, we have developed a reliable operating philosophy, established a credible reputation in the community, and achieved a degree of financial success.

Before beginning, we sought all available information and references that would help us navigate the maze of store planning and start up. While we were able to obtain much information, most of it was not directly applicable to small business retailing, nor was it specific enough to allow us to foresee and plan for the actual costs and events that materialized. For example, the Small Business Administration (SBA) has a wealth of information and many publications available. However, the government definition of small business covers companies with gross sales in the multiple millions of dollars. Many of the pamphlets simply assume too large a scale of operation to be of any real use to a mom-and-pop retailer. Much of the information relates to manufacturing or service operations, which are far removed from the reality of the small retail store we wanted to start.

We didn't want to use the SBA's retired business executive assistance program — called SCORE — because, frankly, we wanted to do it ourselves, our way, and really didn't want an outsider planning our shop. Ego aside, we also secretly feared that a rational, experienced businessperson might take one look at our plans and immediately fall into a fit of uncontrollable laughter at our ignorance and naiveté. This is not to minimize this resource, as this organization is actually quite helpful and would never make fun of rookies like us. But I guess we were a little apprehensive and perhaps too stubborn to admit we needed help.

In any event, we decided to proceed on our own, at our own pace, and desperately needed a how-to book, perhaps with a plain brown wrapper, that would give us detailed instructions on how to set up shop, without having to go public with our intentions. Alas! With the exception of one simplified accounting and finance handbook, we found no such resource.

While we found plenty of books on business management in general, and others on how to get rich in real estate without investing a cent, you can get this kind of information for free on early Sunday morning television infomercials. This kind of free information is usually worth exactly what you pay for it.

After finding out virtually everything the hard way, by trial and error, I decided to try and fill this void in the information marketplace by writing down our experiences, our methods, and our failures so future entrepreneurs would have some footprints to follow, even though they may sometimes appear to have been left by a drunken sailor.

How to
Use This Book

Retail in Detail is designed to provide detailed, hands-on guidance to anyone who is considering entering the retail field. The book is organized into four main parts that coincide with the steps you will need to follow to open your retail store. In addition, there are some helpful resources provided in the appendices that can be useful in carrying out these steps.

- Part I – Research and Planning describes various aspects of setting up a business that you must consider in advance of doing anything. Once you make the first important decision — whether to open a retail store or not — you will then need to make decisions about what products you will sell, where you will sell those products, and how you will finance the whole venture. Part I will help you with those start-up issues and more.

- Part II – Opening for Business goes into detail about getting your store set up and your doors open for business. Part II discusses everything from naming your business and getting the necessary permits and licenses to getting your merchandise and establishing your stated policies on issues like offering credit, accepting checks, and using layaways.

- Part III – Retail Business Management discusses the business aspects of managing your cash, paying bills, maintaining the book-keeping, keeping track of your inventory, and dealing with the people who you work with in your business — your employees and family members, including your spouse.

• Part IV – The Appendices contains several useful references and resources. If you run across a term that is unfamiliar, you will find the Glossary of Terms in Appendix A helpful. Appendix B, Useful Publications, provides you with lists of useful books, magazines, and government publications. Appendix C, Market, Gift, and Design Centers, lists some of the important market centers located around the country — where you can purchase merchandise for your store. Appendix D, Exhibition Companies and Trade Associations provides even more sources for merchandise.

The information in this book is more than just general statements and principles about business that are available from numerous sources. Instead, this book is much more specific, based on the author's particular experiences in the retail business.

Throughout the chapters, the basic concepts of what you need to do are described in detail and illustrated with examples from the author's business, Homespun Cottage. These examples are set apart and in an italic typeface, as in the example below.

The examples of how we have done things at Homespun Cottage are by no means definitive. Not everything that worked for us will be applicable to your business and circumstances. Be aware also that you are reading a book authored, not by a financial expert, but by an ordinary person whose goal is to provide practical, day-to-day advice on starting and operating a small retail business.

Whenever possible, the material has been organized into an easy-to-use list format, punctuated with round bullets (•). The arrows like the ones below point to:

→ Important points to remember; and

→ Important questions to consider.

The final section of each chapter is devoted to Success Strategies. Here, you will find advice, useful tips, ideas to think about, and summaries of the chapter information.

Several worksheets — included at the end of some of the chapters — are designed to help you organize and plan for your business. These worksheets can be photocopied and used as many times as you need them. Actual samples of many of these worksheets are filled out and included in the body of the chapter.

While every effort has been made to organize this book into a logical sequence, many facets of this business do not always lend themselves to a strict chronology. So, much of this information is organized by subject under the most appropriate chapter heading. Therefore, you should read the entire book before proceeding with your plans. You would never try to put that Christmas toy together without reading the instructions all the way through, would you? Would you?!

❖ Part I ❖

Research and Planning

Chapter 1

Before
You Start

Do You Really Want to Do This?

Before you embark on your venture, you will want to spend plenty of time talking over your idea and doing some soul searching. Remember the song from *The Music Man*, when Robert Preston asks the parents: "Are certain words creeping into your son's conversation; words like 'Swell!' and 'So's your old man?'" Well, check your own conversation and see if certain other phrases are creeping in. If so, beware — the entrepreneurial bug may have bitten you. See which statements below apply to you.

- You want to devote your time and talents to building your own business.
- You are tired of the stress of the rat race.
- You want to be your own boss.
- You want to invest your time and money in an enterprise that will help get the kids through college.
- You want a change in lifestyle.
- You want to get rich quick.

You have probably heard or said all of the above or you wouldn't be reading this book. All of these reasons, and many more, are perfectly good reasons for starting a business, except the last one. Most likely, you will not get rich quick, if ever, unless you just happen to corner the market on ground corn cobs the day before the Surgeon General declares them a cure for obesity.

In reality, you can gradually increase your earnings to help out with the household expenses, and if you are persistent and perhaps a little lucky, you can build your business to fully support your family.

At Homespun Cottage, after more than ten years of operation, we are now approaching the point of being able to support the family, assuming our youngest actually graduates from college this fall. I am still employed part-time outside the business, but we are hopeful that sales will continue to increase — and family expenses decrease — so I will be able to come into the business full-time in the near future.

Eventually, your ideas will finally jell into definite action. As you ponder whether or not to take the plunge, some questions you have to answer for yourself are:

- Do you really want to do this?
- Does your family situation allow you to spend a large amount of time on a business?
- Are your skills and personality suited for retailing?
- Do you have the necessary financial resources?
- What happens if your business fails?

The point at which you stop talking and start doing will vary, but for many people, it seems to occur with some regularity during the much celebrated mid-life crisis period. That is a time when you take stock, decide you are not accomplishing all that you want, determine you are tired of the rat race, and want to chuck it all for life as a beachcomber. Or, perhaps after you take a look at your teenage kids, who are to your money as a vacuum cleaner is to lint, you finally know it is time to start your own business. You may also be stuck in a job or profession that seems to be a dead end, or that is not providing you with the satisfaction or financial rewards you expect from life. Or, you may be one of the increasing number of middle and upper managers who have been laid off or retired early as part of the seemingly endless downsizing of corporate America.

Many publications are available that attempt to help you determine if your personality is well-suited to being in business. But even if you don't show an aptitude for business, you probably won't be deterred by a negative score if you really want to own a business. You can refer to the publications list in Appendix B for availability of materials that can test your aptitude. The Small Business Administration materials are probably as good as any.

This book's aim is not to "psych you out" by making you answer questions, such as "Did you hate your mother?" However, if you are a generally well-adjusted person, who enjoys dealing with people, has average intelligence, and who is not crushed by failure, you probably have the basic psychological equipment for retailing. And, since you have invested a few bucks in this book, you probably are stubborn — or naive — enough to go ahead in spite of any psychologist's opinions regarding your suitability or motivation for entering the retail business.

Do consider very carefully whether or not your temperament is suited to operating a retail business. This book will attempt to give you a truthful portrait of the retail experience, both good and bad, from which you can assess your own aptitude for enduring the retailing life. Before you decide whether you want to go ahead, review the two lists below for an idea of the best and worst aspects of the retail business.

Best Aspects of Retailing

→ Working together as a team, most of the time, and the feeling of ownership of a community enterprise;

→ Meeting and making new friends;

→ Going on buying trips and charging it off as a legitimate business expense;

→ Having a feeling of control over at least a part of your life;

→ Receiving compliments on how nice your shop looks — oohs and ahhs are especially rewarding;

→ Looking over Christmas sales figures;

→ Taking a few bucks out of the business now and then;

→ Learning that most people are basically honest and trustworthy; and

→ Having a sense of accomplishment and pride for a business you started from scratch.

Worst Aspects of Retailing

→ Keeping up with all the bureaucratic paperwork;

→ Putting up with children who pick up and destroy things while mothers blithely ignore them;

→ Dealing with customers who complain about price or think they can make it themselves and blatantly make notes on how to copy your merchandise;

→ Looking over January sales figures;

→ Getting caught in the endless buy-sell-buy-sell cycle;

→ Realizing that your large bank balance is mostly accounts payable;

→ Taking inventory;

→ Putting up the Christmas decorations;

→ Taking down the Christmas decorations;

→ Cleaning the restroom, vacuuming, and dusting — just like at home;

→ Discovering an empty clothes hanger hidden behind a cabinet and realizing that you have been visited by a shoplifter; and

→ Getting that large check back, marked "Insufficient Funds" or "Account Closed."

So, there they are! Only you can decide if these pluses and minuses, taken together, will fit into your vision of your preferred lifestyle. One final word of caution — if you don't enjoy people, including meeting and dealing with them on a daily basis, then retailing is probably not the business for you. If you still think you would like to try it, read on.

Getting Started

Investing your savings in a new venture that, according to statistics, has less than a 50 percent chance to survive two years or more is a scary idea. That fancy word, entrepreneur, really means a risk taker, someone who is willing to gamble that he or she can beat the odds and provide services or goods that will meet the needs or wants of that fickle entity, the consumer; and then gamble that the consumer will shell out enough hard-earned dollars to keep the enterprise solvent.

Starting your own business is not quite like putting your quarter in a slot machine, but there are some similarities. You do have a better chance of controlling the odds if you plan carefully, but keep in mind that the jackpot of success does depend, to some extent, on forces beyond your direct control. Below are several recommended preliminary steps to help you increase your chances of success.

Stop Talking and Start Doing

At some point, you have to stop talking and start doing. Many would-be entrepreneurs talk for years about starting various enterprises, even doing some investigations and making some tentative moves, but always pulling back short of actually committing to a business — sort of like sticking your toe in the water at the beach and drawing back to safety and comfort because the water is dark and cold. If you end up doing this, you could see others actually start businesses you have talked about, and succeed. You can't keep dipping your toes in the water and pulling back; you have to jump in sometime, or get off the beach! If you decide to stop talking and start doing, the rest of this chapter is designed to help you maximize your chances of keeping that shingle out, once you put it out.

Make a Solid Commitment

Your most important step is to really solidify your decision. Obviously, there are several decision points at which you can abort the process without serious financial loss, and prudence dictates that you consider these go/no-go decisions carefully, in light of information you obtain. However, do not enter into this phase of the process with the idea that you can always call it quits if something discouraging turns up. It is very important to make a definite commitment at this stage, and only call it off in the face of serious and multiple problems. You will never succeed at anything if you don't make a decision and stick to it. Rest assured that you will encounter landmines and other unpleasant and unanticipated obstacles, and only the truly committed will have the resolve to continue.

Plan Ahead

IBM's famous slogan, "Plan ahead," was never more applicable than in starting a retail shop. Time, effort, and a few dollars invested in planning will pay large dividends in the future.

It is one thing to jump in the water; it is quite another to jump naked into freezing water, without knowing how to swim. In other words, you should spend the time to become informed about the business

7

you are going to enter, learn how it operates, and thus increase your survival chances. The rest of this chapter describes a systematic approach to the planning process.

Set your goals. As mentioned above, most of you, in all probability, have talked about starting a business for years, without actually making any serious commitments in that direction. After you actually make a decision to open a store, set yourself a timetable so that you have plenty of time for research and preparation, but not so far into the future that you will not take the commitment seriously. For example, set a goal of opening about five months in the future, and schedule your activities to meet that date.

Read up on business. Begin by visiting your local bookstores and libraries to find books and magazines that deal with your proposed area of business. You have obviously already taken this advice or you wouldn't be reading this book.

Call or visit your nearest Small Business Administration (SBA) office and obtain current publications and information. Some of the offerings are free although there are some that you will have to purchase. The SBA also offers seminars on small business that will provide a useful orientation. The SBA seminars are very helpful in providing you with a general sense about going into business.

A list of books and magazines, including the SBA's publications, on retailing and small businesses is included in Appendix B. If you can't find these locally, subscribe, purchase, or write for sample copies. As mentioned earlier, there are not many references that will give you the detailed, specific data you will need — other than this publication, of course — but it is helpful to study the magazines and books related to small businesses in general, and the materials on business operations that are closely related to retail.

Research the local business climate. You will want to know as much as possible about the business community in which you will do business. If you are planning on starting your business in a locale other than where you live and with which you are familiar, you can obtain valuable information from travel and regional magazines and books. You should also write or visit the chamber of commerce in your target city and ask for information on the business activities, major industries, schools, and anything else you believe will give you some insight into the business climate in which you will be operating. A wise move is to subscribe to the local newspaper, which can give you information on space availability, costs, and the state of the local economy. In short, a few dollars and a little effort expended in this type of research can yield large dividends of information.

Don't expect the information you want to be indexed and catalogued to your specific needs. You will have to spend many hours digging it out and interpreting it as it relates to your business plans. Real estate agents and such will sometimes offer to do your research for you. This is okay, but don't get lazy and totally rely on this information because, even if it is technically correct, it is designed to sell property or rent space, not ensure that your business is successful. That is your job, and you can't get out of it!

Contact government agencies. Call your local IRS office and arrange to attend one of its free seminars on small business tax matters. By attending, you may receive some valuable information on the kinds of taxes you will have to pay, but you may not be particularly impressed with the quality of the presentation.

Also contact state and local government agencies to find out about registration requirements, permits, and local taxes. Most states have a one-stop business assistance center or economic development department, either of which can help you get started with your paperwork and find your way through the red tape.

One useful publication you should consider purchasing is from a series of books titled *Starting and Operating a Business in ....* This series has a title for each state and the District of Columbia. In addition to providing general explanations of your state's laws, each book lists the current phone numbers and addresses of the state agencies you will need to contact. See the Appendix at the end of this book for information on how to obtain this book and other helpful publications.

Talk to other similar businesses. One of the best ways to become informed is to visit shops similar to the kind you want to start and operate. Look around, write down your impressions, and ask questions of the shop owner if possible. A word of caution here! Don't go into shops in the same area in which you plan to locate and expect merchants to spill their guts to you on how to compete with them. Ask questions only in areas far enough away that you will not be in competition.

The best method is to approach the owners directly, be honest about your intentions, and ask for their advice. Assure them of your intentions not to compete in their sales area. Most retail shop owners will help you with plenty of useful information if they are approached in a nonthreatening way. After all, who doesn't like to talk about their business? This may be the most fertile ground for good information, although it does take more effort to seek out and obtain. Write down your questions before you talk to the shop owners, and take time to jot down the answers as soon as possible after or even during the conversation. Otherwise, you will tend to lose information in the excitement of the moment.

Start figuring out the costs. Survey your area to get an idea of space availability and costs. You can do this by checking your newspaper or calling a commercial leasing agent. This is discussed in more detail in Chapter 4, but now is the time to get acquainted with general space availability and cost.

Success Strategies

If you are going into business as a husband and wife team or with a partner, it is helpful to divide up these preliminary duties according to the interests and skills of the individuals. For example, if you have aptitudes and training in management and finance, while your partner is more creative and imaginative, divide up the responsibilities along those lines. That way, you can divvy up some of these chores and cover more ground in a shorter period of time.

Now that you have decided that retailing suits your needs and lifestyle, and you have done your research and your homework in checking out the territory in your chosen area of operation, it is time to get down to specifics and get that store open.

Chapter 2

Choosing
Your Product Line

How to Decide What You Will Sell

As you look around at the seemingly limitless array of products available for sale in even the smallest town or city, you may be overwhelmed by the task of choosing your products. Or you may find that you must constantly identify and discard products or product lines. Don't dismay! Both aspects are a necessary part of your search for a product line that meets the needs of your proposed customers, as well as suits your own abilities to secure and market it.

In order for your store to be successful, your product line must meet three critical tests. It must:

→ Be merchandise for which a demand exists or can be created;
→ Suit your own talents and abilities to obtain and market it; and
→ Be profitable, especially after taking into account the competitive environment.

Each of these three critical elements and how they relate to product line selection are discussed in this chapter.

Consumer Demand

First, examine the question of demand. As mentioned above, demand can already exist, or it can be created. Catering to an existing demand requires less effort at marketing, but usually involves more competition for consumer dollars.

Take, for example, the home video market. Obviously, a demand exists, but for most areas of the country, the neighborhood video stores have succumbed to heavy pressure from the developing larger chains. Therefore, if you are to be successful with this product, you will have to work hard at providing personalized or special services that are not available elsewhere in your area, or you will have to compete on price, reducing your profitability.

On the other hand, creating a new market is more difficult and requires more advertising and education of consumers, but offers the advantage of a captive market, at least until other retailers realize you are successful and start to compete with you. Be aware that competition will be inevitable when you develop a successful new market.

Creating a market is done most often by importing a product or product line to your area from another area, where it has already proven to be a good seller. Be careful here, though, because a regional product may not be readily transplantable. Microwave grits or hominy may not find ready acceptance north of the Mason-Dixon line. Or, it may take too long to build the market in your area.

Before we started Homespun Cottage, we considered a large number of products, from frozen yogurt to fabrics, before we settled on our final choice. Once we decided on our product line, we then found out the hard way about the regional nature of merchandise when we attempted to introduce new lines of country products, which were popular on the East Coast, to the Southwest. We found that consumers just weren't educated enough in the new looks to make them profitable. Also, some styles and looks are just not transferable. For instance, we have found that certain California products seem to only appeal to Californians, perhaps because of unique lifestyles and environment. Most of these nontransplantable products seem to fall in the decorating, furniture, and ethnic foods categories.

Some products seem to be readily transferable, such as kids' toys, novelty and health foods, and entertainment products. If, on your visits to other parts of the country, you see a product that is popular in a couple of diverse cultures, it probably will sell in your area, and you should consider it a likely candidate. Such products generally require that you move promptly to introduce them, or someone will beat you to the punch.

We had this happen to us with frozen yogurt. We were living in Tennessee, and on a visit to Arkansas discovered the frozen dessert when it was first being introduced. We fooled around so long in making our decision that someone else opened a store nearby, while we were still agonizing. It has been very successful, too. He who hesitates is lost, especially when you are dealing with a hot new product.

Some products for which you create a market are those that are introduced in one locality, and then move across the country in waves, following general fashion trends. You will find it easier to spot this type of product line if you have moved from one region of the country to another. In this circumstance, you have the advantage of broader experience, and more objectivity in identifying a market.

This wave-like movement has been a noticeable phenomenon in the country look. Most country and craft trends seem to begin in the Carolinas, Tennessee, and in California, and then move slowly inland. So, sometimes, it is a matter of introducing a product before its time has come. If you have the patience and market your product aggressively, using magazines and other means to show its acceptance in other areas, you may be successful in accelerating the process. With other items, you may be better off waiting until the trend catches up with your location.

For a new store, you will be wise to stick to known sellers for most of your stock and worry about becoming a trendsetter after you are well-established. In any event, you should keep up with trends in other parts of the country so you can introduce new products when the time is ripe. The best scenario occurs when you can identify a product line that is selling well in your town, but which is only available in a small part of the retail trade area. Then you have the opportunity to market a known seller, without having excessive competition.

This is how we decided on a product line. In late 1984, we moved to Austin, Texas from eastern Tennessee. Susie was interested in country decorating and crafts, and had sold handmade products in seasonal shows in Tennessee. Upon our arrival in Texas, she quickly discovered that there were only two small outlets for these products, and these were confined to two major shopping malls. Austin was booming at the time, and many people were moving in daily. Although the economy has since gone through a major bust cycle, the demand for our products has remained strong.

Obtaining and Selling Products

In addition to consumer demand, the second essential ingredient for product selection is your ability to secure and market the product successfully. Even though you have identified a product that is a proven seller, and it has not yet saturated the market, you will not be successful if you can't get it or if you don't have the talents, knowledge, and skills to market it.

If we had not had Susie's skills and talents in selecting, displaying, and marketing country decorating accessories, we could not have succeeded. Be very careful in this regard.

Whether you are selling fertilizer or furniture, it is important that you know, understand, and be enthusiastic about the product and its uses, and that you are able to relate this knowledge and enthusiasm to your customers. You may be able to get the training and knowledge from your suppliers, but only you can supply the enthusiasm and innate talents necessary to sell your product successfully.

The competitive environment is another subject that deserves a little more consideration when choosing a product you feel you can successfully sell. While it is important to move quickly to be on the cutting edge of a new product or trend, it is also important to consider the likelihood of future competition from larger retail superstores and whether or not you can continue to compete successfully.

14

For example, as mentioned earlier, the home video market was originally dominated by mom-and-pop operators. But since the popularity of the product has become obvious, the field is fast being taken over by giant video stores operated by large retailers, who have the advantage of strong financing and staying power. Therefore, it is a bit of a paradox, but a new product may be too hot if it is likely to prove so popular that it attracts the interest of the industry giants.

However, if you can, you should still consider taking advantage of an emerging product. After all, David slew Goliath, and there are various ways to compete other than on price and volume. But you may wish to evaluate a more established, broader-based product line as opposed to sinking your savings in a single, hot, new item. Of course, if you have the financing, there is nothing to keep you from becoming the giant of a new industry. Don't automatically discard an opportunity to get in on the ground floor — just evaluate the possibilities carefully.

As the fellow who quit his job grading potatoes said, "It is not the work, it is all those decisions!" The road to successful retailing is fraught with many critical decisions that only you can make, so it is important to analyze every aspect of each situation carefully. But it is also important to make a decision promptly and proceed to the next one. Don't become paralyzed and fail to act.

Profitability

Assuming you have now identified a product or line of products for which a substantial demand exists, and which is not flooding your market area, there is one final test and the third essential ingredient for product selection — profitability.

It doesn't matter that you can sell a thousand widgets a day if you can't buy and sell them at prices that will generate a reasonable profit margin.

For example, suppose you decide to open a bait shop to sell worms at your local fishing lake. There is a big demand and little competition. You estimate you can sell 100 boxes of worms a day. However, they will cost you $1.50 a box, and local fishermen are only willing to pay $2.00 a box for them. Rent and overhead will run about $30.00 a day, which means that your net profit of $20.00 a day is not sufficient to keep you in business, even though sales are good. Don't overlook profitability in your search for a product line.

Other Product Selection Issues

Your choice of a product to market has a decided effect on your expenses, your space requirements, your need for employees — both number and degree of training — and the location you will need. If you choose to sell computers, for example, you will need to hire employees with specialized knowledge and training, and you will probably need to provide customer training and software. This will make it more difficult to find and keep qualified employees and require you to provide a broader range of services than, say, an ice cream shop. However, you will need more help in an ice cream shop, and dealing with unskilled and younger employees carries its own set of problems.

Of course, you can always move in different directions with products after your store opens, provided the new products are compatible with your location and space. Although some diversification is healthy, do not to try to cover too much of the waterfront. You have heard the old saying: "Jack of all trades, master of none." You may wind up in that situation if you try to include too great a variety of products and become known as a junk shop.

We are very careful about the kind and quality of merchandise that comes into our shop. We are not a "high-end" gift shop, nor are we a dime store. We try to target the middle-class consumer, including young married couples who may not have large incomes, but specific tastes and desires, nonetheless. We try to keep most items in the $5 to $50 price range, while maintaining a good quality product that doesn't look mass produced or imported. We also stick pretty closely to the country theme.

Success Strategies

Obviously, trends and tastes come and go, and you have to stay up on current trends and move to other product lines when necessary. Your best strategy is to stake out a reasonably well-defined product line and stick to it, unless your market deteriorates. You can experiment with some products that are outside your general area, but only when they are compatible, of good quality, and there is a perceived demand from your current customers. When you experiment with new products, only bring them in on a limited basis, allot them a small amount of space, and carefully gauge your customers' reactions to them.

In summary, the products you select should be:

↦ Products that you know and are enthusiastic about;

↦ Products that are demonstrated sellers in areas similar to yours;

↦ Products for which your market is not saturated; and

↦ Products that will generate sufficient profits to enable you to stay in business.

While this list of criteria for your ideal product line is much easier to write than for you to do, there is no substitute for investing adequate time and energy in this selection process. Of such effort and persistence successful retailers are made.

Chapter 3

Choosing
Your Location

Selecting a General Location

Everyone has heard — and gotten tired of — that old realtor's cliché about the three important aspects of real estate being location, location, and location. While location is a very important part of the retail business, it may not always be crucial in determining success or failure. Even if your circumstances cause you to choose a less-than-ideal location, you can always choose to relocate your store after you are established and have a better sense of your needs in terms of space and location.

Due to the extreme shortage of retail space at the time we went into business, we were forced to locate in a somewhat remote strip center at the edge of town. In spite of this marginal location, we were able to build a loyal clientele because of our product and by using minimal advertising and word-of-mouth publicity. We have since relocated our first store to a strip center at a major intersection where there is a major chain supermarket. This relocation did result in increased sales of from 10 to 20 percent, thus validating the importance of location. However, we were able to relocate during a depressed rental market, at a reduced rent.

Often, relocating will not lower your expenses, and the increased sales volume of a better location may be partially or totally offset by increased costs. This is especially true of some major shopping mall locations, where rents can be exorbitant. It is important to look beyond increased sales to the ultimate goal of higher profits when you are considering locations.

In today's mobile society, consideration of location can literally involve a global search. Although a business can be established successfully in the place where you have lived all your life, it seems that the growth of entrepreneurship is a result of the exposure of more and more people to different areas and cultures. In other words, if you have lived in several different places in this country, you will have had the opportunity to see successes and failures of many different types of businesses in varied settings. Exposure to different places and cultures can also sometimes give you the edge in spotting a product or service that will be successful. See Chapter 2.

The point is not that you have to be a world traveler to establish a successful business, but that there are literally hundreds of choices for locating a business, largely because of the mobility of our society. So, if the world is your oyster, how do you go about narrowing it down? The answer suggested here is to select your location from the outside in, so to speak, based on your own particular circumstances, needs, and personal preferences. That is, decide on a country, state, region, city, neighborhood, and address, in that order. While it is entirely possible to establish businesses in other countries, most would-be retailers reading this book will choose a location in the United States, although the principles involved in locating in another country will be the same.

You will probably choose your present location simply because you are there and are already familiar with the economy and the area. Or, you may be looking to return to the place of your roots, possibly after retiring, to establish a business among your childhood friends and their families. Then again, you may simply want to move to a new area to be near children and grandchildren, escape the cold or heat, live in the mountains or on the beach, or satisfy a score of different personal reasons.

Familiarity Leads to Success

Whatever your reasons are for choosing a location, if you choose a place with which you are not currently familiar, it is imperative that you spend some time in the new location to become oriented. Notice that the term, currently familiar, was used here. Many people assume they know the place where they grew up, even though they have been gone many years.

People and places change, so before you decide to open a toy store in your old neighborhood, better check to be sure the neighborhood still has kids, rather than senior citizens. Furthermore, other more subtle changes can occur, which can have an impact on your business. The population that used to love ice cream and hot dogs may now be on a low-cholesterol, low-fat diet. Or, conversely, they may still thrive on traditional foods, while the rest of the world is on a health kick.

All this is to say that you should get familiar with the proposed location of your new business. If you don't live there, visit and spend time with the people, get to know their wants and needs. You may be able to spend your vacation in the area, or preferably, make several shorter visits at different times of the year.

Try to determine if you will be happy living there. If you are not content, your business will suffer. Many people have returned to their hometown, only to find they didn't fit in anymore. Remember Thomas Wolfe's quote, "You can't go home again." It is also possible that the weather, which seemed pleasantly warm from your vantage point in the snow belt, is actually miserably hot once you get there. In short, don't let the warm glow of nostalgia color your perception of reality. Remember, you must plan for the future, not for the past.

Personal Lifestyle Needs

Don't ignore your own personal lifestyle needs in choosing a business location. Many of the hot spots for new retail opportunities are in resort areas or in new or restored, downtown "festive retail" centers designed to cater to the convention or tourist trade. These two possibilities are opposites in the rural and urban spectrum, and you will need to evaluate your environmental desires in this regard.

Many of these situations are also seasonal, with short, frantically busy periods, followed by the doldrums. Does this pattern fit in with your vision of your preferred lifestyle? Can you handle the pressure of the peak selling season, and perhaps just as importantly, can you handle the periods of inactivity and boredom?

Objective Criteria

Once you have chosen a state, region, and city, it is time to focus on the specific neighborhood in which you will locate. This will involve more detailed and objective criteria, as opposed to the more general and subjective process of choosing an area in which to live.

One of the keys to retail success is traffic, both vehicular and pedestrian. While you can survive in a good vehicular location alone if you have a good product, it is much better to have significant walk-by traffic, as well. The first step is to identify those streets and highways that carry large traffic volumes. You can get this information for free, or for a nominal copying charge, from your city traffic engineering department or your state's highway department. Also, chambers of commerce often have this data available.

The best way to analyze this traffic volume information is to get a city or area map and mark the high-traffic corridors. Then, get in your car and drive these corridors, noting any especially favorable or unfavorable locations. This will enable you to stake out the general areas that seem most favorable for your shop location. Having identified potential high-traffic corridors, evaluate them using the following criteria.

Proximity to large groups of potential customers. A high-traffic highway may not be a good location if it is simply a conduit between two distant inhabited areas.

General availability of space for retailing. Even if you identify a good location, it doesn't do you any good if you can't locate there. Look around for places you can rent.

Customer income levels. By this time, you should know what your product line and price range will be, so it is important to match it with an appropriate customer base. You wouldn't want to locate a fur salon in a neighborhood of factory workers or a bait shop in a ritzy area. Common sense should serve you well here.

Another factor to consider here is disposable income. A store selling discretionary items may not do well in an area of high incomes if everyone is mortgaged to the hilt and has little disposable income. This is not easy to evaluate.

Your best bets for this information are shopping center demographic materials, your local chamber of commerce, and knowledge you gain from actually living in an area. The U.S. Census Bureau has some helpful data, but it may be as much as ten years old if it is near the end of the decade.

Proximity to competitors. While locating near competitors can be advantageous in some situations, such as resort and theme areas, moving next door to an established direct competitor is not usually a great idea. Some overlapping of product lines is okay and can produce a synergistic effect, and some businesses, such as auto dealers, now purposely locate together to profit from a larger customer pool.

Your own convenience. This is an important consideration since one of the reasons for starting a store is to improve your lifestyle and get out of the rat race. If you wind up fighting traffic morning and night, and you have to work in an unsafe or undesirable area of town, you might not be any better off. Your flexibility and your point of residence can be factors here.

In our decision to locate a store, the last factor of proximity to home weighed heavily. Since Susie was to run the store, she decided it was important to be relatively close to home to avoid long drive times through heavy traffic. Also, we had some knowledge of income levels and disposable income in our part of town, which was growing rapidly at the time, ensuring a supply of new potential customers, or so we thought. In actuality, the economy in our city went bust about two years after we opened, and the stream of in-migration turned to out-migration, almost overnight. This could have proven fatal to our business if we had not been located on a major traffic artery, and had we not built up a loyal customer following before the downturn.

Another surprise came when we discovered, shortly after we signed the lease, that our street was scheduled to be widened and rebuilt. Fortunately, we were able to complete our lease term and relocate before the work began. Always check with your local roadway officials before locating since a major project can disrupt traffic for years and sound the death knell for a small business.

Two important points are apparent when you examine Homespun Cottage's experience. First, it is absolute folly to assume that things will stay as they are. The national economy is driven by forces that have not even begun to be understood by economic experts, let alone amateurs. So, expect the unexpected, be flexible, and be prepared to roll with the punches because you will take some hits.

The second point to emphasize is that you can survive in adversity if you do not put all your eggs in one basket, from a location perspective. Try to choose a place that has both high-traffic volumes and a substantial resident population nearby.

Now that you have narrowed the general location down to a specific area, you can search for just the right site for your shop. The remainder of this chapter gets even more specific and gives you some tips on finding that perfect location.

Specific Site Selection

Once you have gotten the general area identified, you can get down to the detail work of finding an affordable location that will provide you an attractive place to transform your inventory into sales and more importantly, profits. Important considerations for selecting a site are:

- Zoning compatibility
- Compatibility with neighboring merchants
- Special atmosphere requirements
- Space requirements
- Costs for space and rules of lessors
- Customer traffic

Zoning Compatibility

Visit your local zoning authority — obtain zoning maps and request a list of the allowable uses in each zoning category. Explain in detail to the zoning official what you will be selling, and obtain, preferably in writing, a list of zones in which you are allowed to operate. Zoning is usually handled by the planning department in most cities and counties.

If this seems like a waste of time, be assured that it is not. Many business plans and even operating businesses have been ruined by running afoul of these laws. It doesn't matter that another business has operated in a certain location for years since most zoning law provisions are only invoked when someone complains. Many older businesses are also "grandfathered" until they cease operating, by virtue of having been there when the laws were passed. All it takes is a disgruntled neighbor to shut you down if you haven't checked carefully. Besides, you don't need to be called out on a technicality when there are so many fun ways to go broke on your own!

If the perfect location for your shop does not have the proper zoning, all is not necessarily lost. All cities and counties have provisions for rezoning property. In some jurisdictions, this is a straightforward and simple process, but in most places, it involves a complicated, time-consuming, and expensive ordeal.

Rezoning or obtaining variances can also become emotional and very unpleasant if your neighborhood chooses to oppose the change. Under these circumstances, you may win the zoning battle but lose your clientele through alienation. Unless the process is simple and you will have no opposition, the best advice is to skip it and find another space. Hell hath no fury like a neighborhood that believes your business will lower property values or interfere with the residents' way of life!

Compatibility with Neighboring Merchants

Next, consider compatibility with other shops in your potential location. Compatibility does not mean whether you have the same astrological sign, race, or religion as the other shop owners, but whether or not you will be able to share, to some extent, the customer base of your neighbors.

Both our shops are located in mid-size retail strip centers, which also contain supermarkets, family haircutting shops, restaurants, a pool chemical store, dry cleaners, a dentist, a national chain retailer, a yogurt shop, and assorted other general retail shops, plus several empty spaces. So far, the customers of the other businesses in the centers are also potentially our customers to some degree, although some of them, such as the pool supply store, cater mainly to men, and our primary customers are women.

Of course, you should be wary of some situations. If you are planning a Christian bookstore, for example, you probably should steer clear of a center filled mostly with businesses selling liquor, adult books, sexual paraphernalia, and other products and services not generally directed at the churchgoing crowd. That is an extreme example, but you get the picture.

Another question is whether or not to locate in the same center or area with a shop in the same generic business. For example, if you plan a gift shop, should you locate in a shopping center with another gift shop? Generally, the answer depends more on the specific product lines, styles, and orientation than on the generic name. For example, a shop that carries gifts, decorating accessories, furniture, cards, and other items that are mostly handmade in a "country" motif will have virtually no overlap with a typical card shop that also carries gifts and similar items, but in a different decorating style. In fact, locating together could actually result in increased sales for both shops by attracting a larger customer pool that may be interested in both lines of products. But, even though this makes sense to you, don't assume the other shop owner will agree.

Most shopping centers have agreements not to lease space to a competing business, and the tenants may be able to exclude you. You might avoid being blackballed by visiting with potential competitors and agreeing not to compete directly on main product lines.

We were turned down because of this type of lease agreement at one shopping center we wanted to locate in. We were unable to convince the other shop owners that our operations would be compatible.

Special Atmosphere Requirements

Does your product line require a special atmosphere in which to be displayed, or can it be sold from a plain vanilla space, off simple racks? This can be an important consideration, although there are ways to overcome this factor through innovative displays, which are discussed in more detail in Chapter 6.

Which is more important — location or atmosphere? Given the choice of location or atmosphere, you would almost always choose location, since a perfect atmosphere won't be enough if you can't get people there. But consider trying to get your lessor to agree not to rent adjacent spaces to a business that would destroy your atmosphere. For example, your rental library business may not flourish next to a bowling alley. Most lessors are sensitive to these situations and try to accommodate reasonable requests. Anyway, it doesn't hurt to ask.

Since we wanted to open a country decorative accessories shop, our first choice was an old historic house that would be compatible with our products and facilitate displaying them. Unfortunately, such a place could not be found in the area we had targeted as being our market area, so we chose location over atmosphere and created our own selling environment.

Space Requirements

How much space do you need? This varies considerably, based on the kind of store, its location, and the cost of the space. If you choose a high-dollar location, such as a mall, you may wish to reduce the space somewhat, use virtually all of it for sales, and rent storage space at a cheaper location. This will save some overhead, but it will be a hassle to shuttle merchandise back and forth, unless you plan your stocking carefully. The way to handle this option, if your rent is very high, is to rent a mini-storage warehouse to store off-season merchandise and displays. Do not, however, try to keep current stock in the warehouse.

Chapter 4 gives some guidelines for estimating inventory costs per square foot. Using these and other data for your particular merchandise line, you can determine about how much space you will need and can afford, initially.

The shape and orientation of the space you choose can be a substantial factor in its usefulness for your particular purpose. Try several possible store layouts on graph paper to see if the space will lend itself to an attractive and functional selling area. A long narrow space may give enough total area, but be unsuitable for display and traffic flow. On the other hand, a square-shaped space may not permit you

27

to divide up the area in room settings, or other special arrangements, if your display scheme requires it.

A space that is about two or three times as deep as it is wide provides a very workable framework for most merchandise displays. If you are going into a new center, you can generally choose as much or as little width as you need, but the depth is normally fixed by the overall building depth. The width is determined by partitions, which are not usually constructed until the space is leased. Don't overlook the Americans with Disabilities Act, which imposes certain requirements for access and restrooms. These requirements must be considered in laying out your space.

For our first gift shop, we started with 1,000 square feet, of which about 300 was devoted to storage, workspace, and restroom, with the remainder in sales area. This proved to be about right, to start with, since our funds for inventory purchases were limited. We have now expanded to 1,500 square feet in the first store, with 1,250 devoted to sales space, and 250 in storage, workshop, and restroom. Our second store began with 1,200 square feet, which we recently expanded to 1,400 square feet.

Costs for Space and Rules of Lessors

A new business needs to keep its overhead down, and your biggest single expense item will almost surely be your rent. Therefore, it is appropriate to pay plenty of attention to this item — not to the exclusion of all else, particularly location, but your attention is definitely justified. However, you also should be concerned about how the lessor's rules will impact your business, and you, personally.

The costs for space and rules of lessors for retail spaces are two items that are strongly related to each other. You will discover that the more expensive a space is, the more likely it will have stricter rules. You will need to evaluate any site with both of these factors simultaneously in mind.

Retail spaces can be divided into four basic cost and rules categories, each option having pros and cons. In ascending order of cost, the four categories are:

- Your own home
- A converted residence
- A retail strip center
- A shopping mall

Your own home. Unless you plan a very modest business, are unusually located, and don't mind people trampling through your domicile, your home is usually out of the question. It is, however, cheap, and might do the job in very unusual circumstances, for example, if you start a bed and breakfast inn, perhaps even with its own gift shop.

A converted residence. A converted residence, such as an historic home or another freestanding structure, may be a viable option for certain types of stores in some locations, and should be thoroughly explored. If the location is isolated from other businesses, you lose some traffic potential, but the reduced cost could offset this, and if the savings are invested in advertising, could actually result in greater profits.

Since you will likely be dealing with an individual owner with this type of space, you may achieve a lower rent, but you may also end up with little support for maintenance and difficulty in getting repairs completed in a timely manner. This type of rental space will likely have few, if any, rules with which to deal, compared to commercial retail centers. A disadvantage will be that you usually must accept the space in its present configuration, which will limit your options for display. Look at the possibilities and see if it will work for you.

A retail strip center. A retail strip center is a more expensive space potential and, as you might expect, has its own set of pros and cons. While generally more expensive than the options discussed above, it will almost always bring you into contact with more potential customers. However, you are very likely to have more rules and regulations. Strip centers usually have professional managers who can provide better maintenance and repair, and who sometimes provide newsletters and group advertising opportunities for tenants. They also generally have structured lease provisions and little flexibility in dealing with you.

In the retail strip center, you will have to comply with rules about such things as signs and sidewalk displays. Most of these rules are for the general good of the tenants, but are restrictive, nonetheless.

In bad economic times, these centers are not immune to financial problems and are prone to bankruptcy, resulting in management and ownership changes that affect the center's viability. If you decide to locate in one, try to choose one with a national or regional manager that has a reputation for stability.

In our present locations, we are in centers managed by large national companies, and we have gotten very good maintenance and upkeep of the center property. However, we have many rules to comply with and a lease that is half-an-inch thick, most of the provisions of which are written to protect the center owner.

A shopping mall. The ultimate American institutions and ideal locations are in major shopping malls. These are also the most expensive and restrictive of all the options. Most have rigid requirements for tenants regarding days and hours of operation, contributions to mall advertising campaigns, and deliveries.

If you want to retain total independence in the operation of your business, malls may not be for you. They do, however, usually produce the highest sales volume, although not necessarily the highest profits, given the premium rental rates demanded. Along with all of the rules, the fast-paced environment may be more than you want to handle initially.

Another major disadvantage is with deliveries if you have bulky items to sell. Malls usually have restricted access for vendors, and your customers, leaving with merchandise, experience the same problems. Unless you are an anchor tenant, like Sears or J.C. Penney, you are unlikely to have direct sidewalk access. However, even with these drawbacks, for some businesses, the mall is the best place to be and should be strongly considered.

Customer Traffic

When you select your site, considering customer traffic is really not a stand-alone issue since it is interrelated with the other factors. It must be kept in mind, however, since it may be the most important factor to the success of your business. Even though you may have the best-shaped, least-expensive, best-located space in town, if you don't have a substantial number of customers for your type of merchandise coming by your store, it will profit you little. For example, if you are selling ultra modern furniture, it probably wouldn't be a good idea to locate in a center surrounded by historic homes.

To ensure adequate customer traffic, you will have to make some observations and do research as to the kinds of customers who typically come to the particular shopping area you choose.

Most retail centers have a package of demographics they will provide to you. If they don't offer it, ask them for it. These packages typically contain information on the number, average income, and makeup of households within a one-mile and five-mile radius. They will tell you, for example, how many households are single or married couples, whether they have children, and the range of ages of the residents.

Spend some time analyzing this data to see if the existing customer base contains the kinds of people who are likely to buy your products. For example, your ideal customer profile might be described as married couples, preferably homeowners, with disposable incomes that will allow them to purchase gifts, furniture, and decorating accessories for their homes or for their friends and families. You will also want to define your preferred age group, such as people between the ages of twenty and fifty-five.

By comparing your ideal customer profile to the information provided by the retail center, you can make a more informed decision about locating there. It will take a little digging, but a thorough perusal of the demographic data can yield valuable insights into your potential customer pool.

Negotiating Your Lease

Once you have selected the right location, it is time for the dreaded lease negotiations. It can be as simple as buying a toothbrush, or as complicated and distasteful as buying a new car, complete with the playing of "the game" to settle on a final price. Obviously, the process is simpler if you are dealing with an individual owner who is very flexible, or a large corporation that has policies against negotiations. The results can be very different in these two extreme cases, but it can be very simple, as in, "Take it or leave it."

Most of the time you will be dealing with a leasing agent or a shopping center manager, and in that case, you will have some room for negotiation. The amount of leverage you have will vary greatly with the economy and the retail vacancy rate in your area.

> *Our first lease in a small, relatively remote, strip center offered us very little room for negotiation on price because of the boom economy and the extreme shortage of retail space. We were, however, able to secure some concessions on the lease terms, as recommended by our attorney.*
>
> *Our second lease was negotiated in a lean economy, with retail space going begging, and we were able to gain major concessions on price, although the major national firm we were dealing with was somewhat inflexible on its standard lease agreement terms.*

You should, by all means, have an attorney review your first lease, but don't let your lawyer make your decisions. Listen to his or her advice, but don't be dominated. Attorneys are paid to point out potential risks, and they may be overly cautious in trying to make sure you don't later blame them for failing to warn you properly. Pay attention to issues your attorney brings up, but make your own business decision, even if it does carry some risks.

Basic Lease Elements

Leases for retail space usually have minimum terms of three years, although shorter and longer terms are sometimes possible. The following elements are usually included in retail space leases, in various combinations.

→ A basic term obligates the tenant to pay for the space for a specific time period, usually three years, whether or not the business survives that long.

→ A basic monthly rental rate per square foot or a percentage of gross sales, whichever is greater, is charged. Typical rents can range from $0.90 to $3.00 per square foot per month, or 6 percent of gross sales, whichever is greater. The percentage rent is figured on annual monthly average sales. Unless your store is super successful, you will probably not reach this threshold during your first lease term.

→ The lessor is normally responsible for maintaining all equipment serving the space including electrical, plumbing, heating, air conditioning, and structural components. This may sound illogical, but it seems to be standard.

→ A finish-out allowance is usually provided to you in return for the three-year term of the lease. The lessor will generally provide you an allowance to finish out the space to your specifications. This is typically in the range of $10–$15 per square foot, which is sufficient for basic walls, ceiling, lighting, electrical, plumbing, heating, air conditioning, and insulation. It does not normally cover wall finishes, carpet and floor tile, signs, and any other custom work to suit your shop's needs. The finish-out allowance amount and coverage is subject to negotiation within a fairly narrow range.

→ Prepaid rent, typically one to three months, is considered standard.

→ A security deposit can range from zero to two month's rent.

→ Water and sewer are usually included in the lease rate, but expect to pay extra for gas, electricity, and trash removal.

→ Triple net charges are monthly charges, usually for taxes, insurance, and common area maintenance, that allow the lessor to pass on these variable costs to you. They are normally adjusted annually and can represent an additional 10–25 percent added to your basic rent.

Triple net charges should not be confused with the insurance, tax, and maintenance costs you will pay as a retail business. They are strictly to repay the owner of the shopping center or other building for his or her costs for these items. They also typically include water and sewer service unless your business will be a high user, such as a restaurant, hair salon, or similar enterprise. These triple net charges are included as a separate item because they vary from year to year, and the landlord wants to be sure they are recovered from the lessees. The fixed amount per square foot lease, the amount referenced above ($0.90 to $3.00 per square foot), is designed to recover the landlord's cost of building the structure, which is usually fixed at the time of completion of construction.

You will have to pay sales and other taxes levied directly on your business. Most landlords will also require you to carry business insurance, which protects you and the landlord from casualty losses and from liability as a result of the operation of your business. You must also maintain heating and air conditioning equipment used exclusively by your business, as well as storefronts and other interior maintenance items.

Negotiating Better Terms

As your first step in lease negotiations, contact the leasing agents for spaces in which you are interested and ask for proposals. After receiving several proposals, you should have an idea of the menu of terms and prices you will have to deal with in your negotiations. At this point, you may find it desirable to engage a leasing agent to negotiate the lease for you if you feel overwhelmed by the task or if you are not a particularly good negotiator. You can do it yourself, however, and by following some basic guidelines, you should be able to achieve reasonable terms. You will do even better if you can locate at least two spaces that can meet your needs, thus ensuring competition for your lease.

After you receive the proposals from the leasing agents or center managers, don't let them pressure you into signing a lease prematurely. Prepare and submit your own counteroffer, in writing, in response to the proposals. Some counteroffer concessions you will want to negotiate are:

→ Lower basic rates;
→ No payment of a percentage of sales, or payment of a smaller percentage;
→ Larger finish-out allowance and coverage of more improvements;
→ Graduated lease rates, starting low but increasing over the lease term;
→ Limits on triple net charges;
→ Inclusion of some utilities in the base rate;
→ Shorter lease term;
→ Escape clauses to allow you to get out of the lease in certain circumstances;
→ Free rent, such as one to six months, depending on market conditions; and
→ Lower prepaid rent and security deposits.

Include several or all of these points in your counteroffer proposal. You are unlikely to succeed with them all, but your counteroffer will establish a good position from which to negotiate and will help you evaluate the willingness of the lessors to engage in meaningful negotiations. Make sure the lessors are aware that you are negotiating with another center. After you feel you have gotten all the concessions you can get, choose the one that is to your best advantage and finalize the terms.

One final word of caution in negotiating: it is possible to be too demanding and distrustful, and thus spoil a relationship that you will have to live with for a long time. You will most likely find that your relationships with landlords will go very well, and many of your fears about problems in dealing with issues not spelled out in the lease will be unfounded. There is still a place for trust in business dealings, and most issues can be worked out when each party approaches them with consideration for the other party.

Success Strategies

Leasing a space is a long-term commitment to consider carefully. Before you sign a lease, make sure you have considered all of the site selection issues in this chapter, both business and personal. Then, once you have decided on a place, the main points to remember when you go about leasing your space are to:

→ Deal with reliable lessors.
→ Try to define the terms as best you can.
→ Have your lawyer review the lease.
→ Proceed with an attitude of trust.

But, before you actually lease a space, you will need to look at how you are going to finance your start-up costs. Financing your business is the topic of the next chapter.

Chapter 4

Financing
Your Business

How Much Money Do You Need?

When you go into the retail business, you will need to develop a diverse set of skills. You must learn to plan carefully, become fully informed before acting, and master dealing with many issues simultaneously. Furthermore, you will find that starting a retail business doesn't fit into a direct sequence. You must plan, do research, and then go back, readjust, and plan again. For example, once you have a pretty good idea of costs, it is logical to do your detailed financial planning at that point. But, it is also critical to consider your financial requirements and capabilities before you begin any detailed planning.

Likewise, you will probably need to flip back and forth through the various parts of this book as you go through the process. You can use this chapter to do your preliminary estimates before you begin your search for a location, and then come back and refine your estimates after you nail down more of the costs.

The costs you will need to consider are divided into two categories — one-time and monthly expenses. To help you begin the task of estimating your start-up costs, you can use the one-time and monthly expense worksheets at the end of this chapter. These two worksheets include lists of items you will need to consider to make your estimates, along with a range of costs you can use as a starting point. These costs will obviously vary, depending on your specific business and location. After you read through this chapter, take some time to fill in the blanks for both of these worksheets.

If you don't have this information, then use the figures from either the instructions for the worksheets or the completed samples featured below. You can translate these costs to your own area, using indexes that are available in the business section of your local library. But these will be close enough for rough estimating purposes. Use the costs in the worksheet instructions and the samples below for the purpose they are intended — to give you some real numbers with which to deal — and not as the exact amounts you should expect to spend.

Your one-time costs are expenditures you will need to make just to get the doors open.

One-Time Costs Worksheet – Sample

Prepaid rent and security deposit	$2,700.00
Triple net charge	324.00
Utility deposits	250.00
Finish-out costs	2,500.00
Sign	2,800.00
Preopening advertising	1,500.00
Initial inventory	19,500.00
Licenses and permits	0.00
Display fixtures	1,000.00
Operating capital	15,552.00
Subtotal	$46,126.00
Contingencies (15 percent)	6,919.00
Total	$53,045.00

One-Time Costs Narrative

The one-time costs in the sample are for an actual business starting in Austin, Texas in 1996. The prepaid rent and security deposit amount is for 1,500 square feet at $0.90 per square foot. The amount shown is for two month's rent ($1,350 per month). The triple net charge is 12 percent of the monthly rent ($162 × 2 months).

The utility deposit is for two months, based on an average of the annual utilities for a similar space. The finish-out costs include materials costs only for wallpaper, wood trim, and special built-in features, with all the labor performed by the business owner. The sign estimate is for what is called a back-lit block-letter sign that spells out the business name (15 letters). It is about 14 inches high. Lessors generally have detailed requirements for signs, along with lists of vendors with approved designs.

Preopening advertising includes six 10-second radio spots during morning or afternoon drive time, one 60-second radio spot, and eight 30-second TV spots during non-prime time hours. The initial inventory for this business — a gift store — came to $13 per square foot (1,500 × $13). The display fixtures are mostly desks and storage racks constructed by the owner. Some of the fixtures being used for display are furniture pieces, so these costs are included in the initial inventory costs since these pieces are for sale.

When we started our business, we bought most of our fixtures at garage sales and flea markets and did most of the carpentry, painting, and wallpapering ourselves. If you have the time and skills to do this, you can keep your costs in the lower end of the ranges cited in the instructions for the worksheets. We also did not hire any employees at first, but added part-time help later on, after our cash flow was established.

Operating capital was calculated from the monthly expense worksheet below. The figure reflects three months operating expenses. Operating capital is added into the one-time costs because it will take awhile for your cash flow to start covering these expenses. Finally, a 15 percent contingency is figured in to cover any unexpected costs or underestimated amounts. This way, you will not find yourself short of money at a critical time.

In addition to your one-time, initial start-up costs, you must also take into account your monthly operating costs and how you will meet those obligations until you get your cash flow going. The sample below shows the monthly expenses for the same business in Austin, Texas.

Monthly Expense Worksheet – Sample

Rent	$1,350.00
Utilities	154.00
Triple net, add-on to lease amount	166.00
Employee wages and salaries	900.00
Payroll taxes (7.65% of wages)	69.00
Sales taxes	1,120.00
Advertising	800.00
Bank charges	175.00
Insurance	50.00
Equipment leases	50.00
Miscellaneous	350.00
Total monthly expense	$5,184.00

Monthly Expenses Narrative

The monthly estimated expenses shown are for a 1,500 square foot gift shop, with two part-time employees working a total of 160 hours. As in the previous example, the rent is $0.90 per square foot, with a 12 percent triple net charge.

Payroll taxes are figured at 7.65 percent of total wages. This represents your share of the federal taxes. You will withhold an equal amount from employees, along with income taxes and remit the total to the IRS. This withheld amount is included in the total wages figure mentioned above.

There are also state and federal unemployment taxes. They usually are minimal and are paid quarterly, so they are not included here. Sales taxes are figured on estimated sales of $14,000, at a rate of 8 percent. In actuality, sales tax is not an expense item, but is a pass-through amount that you collect and remit to the state. However, since you will likely be including the sales tax amount as part of your gross receipts ($14,000 x 1.08 = $15,120) it is included as an expense item for the sake of convenience.

The monthly advertising budget represents about six percent of gross sales for the first few months of operation. After startup, an amount between three and six percent of sales is probably adequate for advertising. See Chapter 9 for more information on setting your advertising budget.

The bank charges are service charges and the discount charges for credit card purchases — about three percent of credit card sales. The business insurance includes basic liability coverage and coverage for losses to your inventory from a fire or flood. The equipment lease charges are for the electronic credit card processing terminal. Expenses such as travel, repairs, office supplies, and magazine subscriptions are included in the miscellaneous category.

After you establish your monthly expenses, estimate your monthly sales so you can do a cash flow projection for your first quarter of operation. Estimating sales for a new retail store is very difficult, and fraught with uncertainties. You can start with a range between $75 and $200 per square foot per year. For most stores, this is not spread equally over the twelve months. For a gift store, a typical monthly sales projection could look as follows for the 1,500 square foot store used in the above example.

Sales Estimate – Sample

January	$ 5,392
February	8,824
March	8,909
April	8,311
May	8,712
June	5,931
July	5,950
August	11,211
September	9,794
October	10,545
November	19,018
December	23,984
Total	$126,581
Average monthly sales	$ 10,548

Depending on the time of year you begin, you can see that sales are subject to a wide variation. You should consider opening mid-year, if possible. Almost all retail sales are lower during the first few months of a calendar year.

Once you have estimated your sales for the first quarter of operations, you can then make a cash flow projection as in the example below.

Cash Flow Projection Worksheet – Sample

	Month 1	Month 2	Month 3
Estimated sales	$8,000	$10,000	$12,000
Monthly expenses	<7,500>	<5,500>	<6,000>
Merchandise purchases to restock*	<4,000>	<5,000>	<6,000>
Monthly total**	<3,500>	<500>	0
Cumulative totals	<3,500>	<4,000>	<4,000>

* Merchandise purchases to restock are figured at your wholesale cost of the merchandise you estimate will sell.

** The monthly total is determined by subtracting "Monthly expenses" and "Merchandise purchases to restock" from "Estimated sales".

This analysis indicates you should budget $4,000 to cover negative cash flow through your first quarter of operation. Use the blank worksheet at the end of this chapter to project your first quarter's cash flow.

If you are confident of your sales estimates, you can use the amount you should budget for from your Cash Flow Projection Worksheet as the figure for the "operating capital" category of the One-Time Costs Worksheet. Otherwise, a more conservative approach is to use three to six months' expenses (the total from the Monthly Expense Worksheet) as your operating capital requirement.

If you have filled out all of the worksheets, you now have a figure that represents the amount of money you will need to start up your business, as well as estimates of monthly operating costs and a projection of your cash flow for the first quarter of operation. You probably need more money than you thought, don't you? Consider this as just another demonstration of Murphy's Law — that everything always costs more than you think it will. This is especially true when you open a business.

Where Will You Get the Money?

Now that you have an educated guess as to the amount of money you will need, you must decide how you will get it. You can finance it from your savings if you have that much, through a personal loan, or with a business loan. If you choose to use your savings, you are using what is known as internal financing. In addition to funds you personally invest, another form of internal financing is using the internally generated cash flow from your operations — which comes later, after you get the business open. Most small businesses must rely on internal financing. The disadvantages of internal financing are the limitations you will face, such as:

⇢ The size of your investment is limited by how much money you have; and

⇢ Funds generated by the business are limited by the size and profitability of your business' operations.

Your other option is to seek external financing. External financing falls into two broad categories — debt financing and equity financing. Debt financing is a contractual arrangement through which you promise to repay the money or credit advanced, plus interest, as in a bank loan. The chief advantage of debt financing is that the creditors have no voice in the management of your business, and the relationship exists only for the duration of the contract.

Equity financing is obtained by selling an ownership interest to an outside investor, such as by incorporating or forming a partnership. Equity financing is extremely difficult to obtain for a retail store unless you have friends or family who are willing to invest with you.

In our case, we chose to use savings and avoid the additional burden of loan payments in our start-up period. We strongly believe this is the best course if you can swing it.

If you need to borrow money, you will struggle to make your loan payments during the first year, and that extra burden can sometimes be the deciding factor in whether your business will succeed or fail. But, the case for using your savings instead of borrowing is more a psychological argument than a financial one, because using your savings costs you in lost interest and can leave you short in an unexpected emergency. However, owing yourself gives you a higher comfort level than owing First National Bank, and you will be more lenient on yourself if you miss a payment!

If you need to borrow, you can explore the following options:

- Life insurance loans
- Personal loans
- Second mortgages
- Business loans

The options above are listed in order of preference because of cost and ease of acquiring. This recommendation may fly in the face of conventional financial advice, but if you are not looking at it from a strictly financial analysis viewpoint, you will see that you can avoid many hassles.

Getting credit established is a good idea, but unless you have a strong relationship with a banker, a new business will have severe handicaps in obtaining start-up financing from a bank. Without a track record, you will probably have to put up considerable collateral to get a loan, so you are better off to use other methods, if possible, at least initially. After you have an operating record, then you can negotiate a line of credit with your bank. So, keep your banker informed about your business and its progress. This will prevent your having to go to an unfamiliar face in the bank to negotiate a loan if you need one to tide you over in a financial pinch.

Success Strategies

This may seem like a short chapter on perhaps the most critical element of starting a business. However, the brevity of treatment is not meant to underemphasize the importance of solid financing. Make sure to use the worksheets on the next few pages, so you have a true picture of how much money you will need.

You will want to make several copies of each worksheet, since you will probably need to pencil this out several times before you finally take action.

If you do not start with enough capital, you will jeopardize the success of your business — and any money you do invest. Furthermore, the struggle you will go through with an undercapitalized business will not be pleasant.

While the advice in this book on financing your business is limited, other books are written by financial experts. If you do not have the financial resources to begin on your own, some good references on this aspect of securing funding for your business are listed below.

→ *Financing Your Small Business: Techniques for Planning, Acquiring & Managing Debt*

→ *The Insider's Guide to Small Business Loans*

→ *The Money Connection: Where and How to Apply for Business Loans and Venture Capital*

→ *Raising Capital: How to Write a Financing Proposal*

→ *Successful Business Plan: Secrets & Strategies*

See Appendix B at the back of this book for a description of these books and ordering information. Here you will also find many other valuable sources of information.

One-Time Costs Worksheet – Instructions

Before you begin, make several copies of the worksheet since you will rework your figures many times.

1. Enter the amount from your lease contract for prepaid rent and security deposit. Or, estimate the amount at one to three months of the average rental rate ($0.90 to $3.00 per square foot/month) for your area. Also figure in the triple net charge.

2. Check with your local utility companies for the amount of deposit they generally charge for retail stores.

3. Your finish-out costs are those that are not covered by the lessor, such as paint, wallpaper, and floor coverings. You can estimate these at between $2 to $5 per square foot.

4. Call a local sign company for prices on different kinds of signs. Depending on what you will need, the price can range from $250 for a modest sign to $5,000 for a large, illuminated sign that can be seen from the highway.

5. Preopening advertising expenses can range from $500 to $2,000. Talk to an advertising agency to plan this expense and get examples of costs for different types of approaches and coverage.

6. Depending on whether your products are larger or smaller, expensive or inexpensive, the range of costs for inventory can vary from $12 to $40 per square foot.

7. Check with local authorities for the costs of business permits and licenses. These costs can vary widely from community to community.

8. The types of display fixtures you will need will depend on your products. For example, furniture needs few fixtures, whereas apparel generally must be hung on racks. Estimate the fixtures at between $2 to $5 per square foot, based on the usual display needs for your product line.

9. Using the Monthly Expense Worksheet on page 49, put in a figure representing from three to six months' operating expenses.

10. Subtotal lines 1 through 9.

11. Multiply line 10 by 0.15 (15 percent) to establish a contingency variable to cover unexpected expenses.

12. Add line 11 to line 10. This total is your one-time costs estimate — basically, what it will take to open the doors.

One-Time Costs Worksheet

1. Prepaid rent and security deposit $_____

    Triple net charge $_____

2. Utility deposits $_____

3. Finish-out costs $_____

4. Sign $_____

5. Preopening advertising $_____

6. Initial inventory $_____

7. Licenses and permits $_____

8. Display fixtures $_____

9. Operating capital $_____

10. Subtotal $_____

11. Contingencies (15%) $_____

12. Total $_____

Monthly Expense Worksheet – Instructions

Before you begin, make several copies of the worksheet, since you will need to rework and readjust your figures as you go.

1. To estimate rent, enter the amount of square feet you will need and the average rate per square foot for your area ($0.90 to $3.00) and multiply.

2. Consult your local utility companies for estimates. If you already have a particular space in mind, the utility company can tell you what the average monthly bills were for past occupants.

3. To determine the triple net charge, add between 10 and 20 percent of the amount of rent (line 1 above).

4. Enter the amount you expect to pay per month for extra help. Determine this by multiplying the number of hours you will require help by the prevailing wage in your area.

5. Multiply your payroll totals from line 4 by 0.0765 (7.65%) to determine payroll taxes for the month.

6. Enter your state's sales tax rate and your estimated monthly sales and multiply.

7. A ballpark figure to use for your monthly advertising budget, which is discussed further in Chapter 9, is between 3 and 6 percent of your estimated sales. This cost will likely fall between $200 and $800 per month.

8–11. Using actual amounts or the figures from the sample in the chapter, fill in the appropriate amounts.

12. Enter the monthly payment amount for your loan or proposed loan.

13. Add lines 1–12 to arrive at your monthly expenses.

Monthly Expense Worksheet

1. Rent _____ sq. ft. X $_____ /sq. ft. $_____

2. Utilities $_____

3. Triple net, add-on to lease amount $_____

4. Employee wages or salaries, if any $_____

5. Payroll taxes $_____

6. Sales taxes (sale tax rate _____% X $_____
   estimated sales)

7. Advertising $_____

8. Bank charges $_____

9. Insurance $_____

10. Equipment leases $_____

11. Miscellaneous $_____

12. Loan repayment, if any $_____

13. Total monthly expenses $_____

Cash Flow Projection Worksheet – Instructions

1. Enter your estimated sales for the first three months. Your sales can range from $75 to $200 per square foot per year.

2. Enter the total monthly expenses from the Monthly Expense Worksheet.

3. Estimate restocking costs at 50 percent of monthly estimated sales.

4. The monthly total is line 1 minus lines 2 and 3 [line 1 – (line 2 + line 3)].

5. The cumulative totals are running totals of the amounts on line 4.

Cash Flow Projection Worksheet

	Month 1	Month 2	Month 3
1. Estimated sales	$_____	$_____	$_____
2. Monthly expenses	$_____	$_____	$_____
3. Merchandise purchases to restock	$_____	$_____	$_____
4. Monthly total	$_____	$_____	$_____
5. Cumulative totals	$_____	$_____	$_____

❖ Part II ❖

Opening for Business

Chapter 5
Planning Your Opening

Chapter 6
Displaying Your Wares

Chapter 7
Setting House Rules

Planning
Your Opening

Details for Opening Your Store

Now that you have your financing lined up and have your space leased, it is time to get down to the serious business of ensuring that when your doors open for business the first day, you have a name, licenses, permits, and something to sell.

Your Store's Name

"What's in a name?" Shakespeare wrote. If he had been in the retail business, he might have answered, "Your destiny." Perhaps that is overstating the case a bit, but a name can be an important asset in identifying and setting your business apart from the competition. A name deserves careful thought, and should, if possible, be descriptive, catchy, and easily remembered.

Be careful not to choose a name that is too close to an existing business' name. Remember the old joke about the grocer who, when cautioned that he could not name his store Piggly Wiggly, chose Hoggly Woggly, instead. You may have also seen news stories about how jealously some national chains protect their names and trademarks, suing any and all who dare to copy. While a name is important, it is not the be-all and end-all of your business.

You will be amazed at how many businesses that sell similar merchandise, both wholesale and retail, use similar words in their names, thus limiting the possibilities for original names. Perhaps it is not so amazing, but it is a fact nevertheless. You will want to search for an original name that evokes instant identification with your merchandise motif.

Do the best you can on the name selection, but don't go into business as a "No-Name Store." Pick something and go with it! After you decide on a name, you must usually register it at your county courthouse or secretary of state's office. This is ordinarily a simple process and will ensure that you don't duplicate another local store name. However, procedures vary from state to state, so check with your local authorities.

We almost got a divorce over this issue! Not really, but Susie did agonize, seemingly endlessly, over the choice of a name. Since we were starting a country gift shop, she wanted the word "country" in the name for obvious reasons. However, there was another shop (not a gift shop) nearby, which had the "C" word in its name and she didn't want to appear to be copying.

She must have tried and discarded a million names. As we neared the point when we had to have a name, the increased pressure only made the name selection more difficult. Finally, she chose, in desperation, "Homespun Cottage," both words of which evoke a country image. This name has served us fairly well, although several people have assumed we were a restaurant, a fabric store, or a needlework shop. By and large, however, it gives the right connotation, and has achieved a reasonable name recognition in our city.

Susie was surprised at the process for registering our name in Austin. She went to the county clerk's office, was told to check several large ledgers to see if the name had been taken, and if not, to enter it in the book. And so it was done. We assumed there would be a computerized process for checking and cross-checking and that we would receive a gilded certificate bestowing our name. It is rather comforting to find that sometimes simplicity survives in the midst of a bureaucratic world.

You will also need a logo for your store to ensure your name recognition. You can either choose a stock logo from your packaging supplier, with your store name on it, or have one custom designed.

> *We chose a local artist — a person with no apparent interest or understanding of our merchandise to design our first logo, but it was rather blah and Susie was never satisfied with it. We later commissioned another artist with an interest in our line of merchandise, who produced a very attractive logo, which we have now adopted.*

It helps if your artist has some interest in your particular line of goods. Using a stock logo is cheaper and quicker, but it is worth the small amount of extra money to get a unique one.

Business Registration

If you live in a state that has a sales tax, you will need a sales tax number and license, which you get from your state tax agency. This is mandatory in order to be able to sell merchandise and collect sales tax, but it is also necessary to be able to purchase merchandise at wholesale and to get into trade shows. Registering your business will get you on the computer that sends out the forms for reporting and remitting sales tax to the state government. In Texas, taxes must be remitted on a quarterly or monthly basis, depending on your sales volume. Your state may have different reporting requirements. Contact your state's department of revenue for more information.

Before hiring employees, you need to apply for an employer identification number (EIN) from the IRS, but don't do this until you are sure you are ready to hire employees, as you will be put on the IRS computer to receive the quarterly tax reporting forms, and they will keep coming for the rest of your natural life.

To apply for an EIN, file a completed *Form SS-4* at the earliest possible time, especially if you will have employees. If you will operate your business as a corporation or partnership, IRS tax law requires you to file *Form SS-4* even if you will have no employees. You will also need to register for paying your estimated income taxes on a quarterly basis.

To help you learn more about your tax responsibilities as a new employer, you can request an *Employer's Tax Guide* and business tax kit from your local IRS office.

You may also need business licenses and special permits from your local government. Check with the planning or finance department of your city or county for information on this. In addition, you may need a state business license to operate your business. Contact your secretary of state's office for more on this requirement.

Don't try to ignore these requirements. They will find you out eventually and cause you serious problems. Better to know about them and plan for them than to ignore and have them come back to haunt you at a very inopportune time.

Business Insurance

The next issue you will want to address is your business insurance. As mentioned in the chapter on leasing your business, your landlord will furnish insurance on the building and most equipment, and pass the cost on to you in the triple net charge. Your lease will almost surely require you to obtain your own insurance, covering losses to your inventory. This policy must usually also cover damage to the lessor's equipment that you are responsible for maintaining. Most importantly, the policy must also protect you and the landlord from liability as a result of operating your business.

Most leases will require that you include the lessor as a named insured and furnish proof of insurance. The cost of this insurance varies with the amount of inventory you cover, your annual sales, the risk zone in which the building is located, age and condition of the building, and other rating factors.

In a modern strip center, located in a city with a good fire department, you can expect to pay a monthly premium of about one-tenth of one percent (0.1%) of your inventory value. For example, if you have sales of about $250,000 per year and an inventory of $50,000, your monthly premium should be somewhere around $50. Check with a local agent for firm quotes.

To learn more about business insurance and how to keep your premiums down, pick up a copy of the book, *The Buyer's Guide to Business Insurance*, available from The Oasis Press. See Appendix B for more information and how to order.

Going to Market

Now that you have a name and several numbers, permits, and licenses, all you need is something to sell. Unless you plan to sell a very specialized product, the best place to gain access to most products is at "Market." These are regional market centers with showrooms similar to retail shops, but these markets sell only to bona fide retailers. Most showrooms represent many companies and individuals with products to sell. Sometimes they are organized along similar product lines, while others feature a more eclectic selection of merchandise.

The major market centers, such as Dallas, Atlanta, Chicago, and Los Angeles, are large complexes with goods ranging from jewelry to furniture. Small regional markets are also scattered throughout the country in larger cities. See appendices C and D for lists of merchandise sources. In addition to the permanent showrooms, most market centers have special shows throughout the year, usually in January, July, and September, during which hundreds of temporary exhibitors display their work.

You cannot take merchandise back home with you from a market. Instead, you place orders for later shipment. In addition to the larger regional market centers, there are also wholesale markets that follow a circuit across the country, featuring a number of products supplied by individual exhibitors. These are particularly numerous in the handmade merchandise fields.

Since markets sell only to retailers, you will be required to produce evidence that you are one. Usually, you must present a sales tax certificate, along with printed checks, letterhead, or business cards in order to gain access as a buyer. You can do this on your first trip, or in advance, through the mail. You will be issued a market card, similar to a credit card, for identification.

Major markets provide a wide range of services to buyers, including reservation services for hotels, airlines, and restaurants, often at commercial discounts. Markets are eager to make life easier for buyers, no matter how large or small the stores they represent. Likewise, the showroom personnel are always friendly and helpful, and willing to assist new buyers.

Your first trip to market should not be during a show, which is always crowded, hectic, and overwhelming, even to experienced buyers. By making your first trip when no show is in progress, the sales personnel will have plenty of time to work with you, answer questions, and generally give you plenty of good advice that can prove extremely helpful.

Most showrooms have sales representatives who will call on you after they learn of your store. These representatives generally are well acquainted with their merchandise and can advise you on best sellers and items that are slow movers. You have to use your own judgment, but it is not a bad idea to listen to their advice because it is not to their advantage to sell you merchandise that will just gather dust on your shelves. The bottom line, though, is that it is your money and your decision.

Some retailers opt not to go to the market centers after they establish ties to several sales representatives. While it is cheaper and more convenient to buy your goods in your own store, it may be a mistake to isolate yourself from the rest of the industry and rely solely on salespersons.

The market centers provide a look at what is happening in your field and help you to keep up with trends, allowing you to stay current with your merchandise and anticipate changing tastes. Overall, the travel costs are well spent, and as a side benefit, allow you to have a sort of busman's holiday, away from the daily selling routine. And, the travel expenses are deductible — most of them, anyway.

When we started our business, our first orders for goods were placed at the Dallas Market Center, probably the largest in this country.

We look forward to our market trips, since they allow us to get away from the shop and our kids and spend some time together, although that time is usually pretty much filled with research and buying. We try to go to different markets to get a broader view of available merchandise and to allow us to enjoy different areas of the country. Buying trips to Boston, Atlanta, Pennsylvania, Indiana, and Tennessee have not only yielded some merchandise exclusives, but have also given us some enjoyable sightseeing opportunities.

Tips for Surviving Market

Buying at a major market center can be an overwhelming experience, unless you plan your activities carefully and purchase your goods in an organized fashion. To give you a better idea of the process, and, hopefully, help you avoid some of the first-time jitters, here are some handy tips to use for a typical market trip.

Begin planning for market trips well in advance. Obvious chores are securing travel tickets and hotel reservations several months in advance since accommodations are usually full during the show. Take advantage of the market center's travel service and stay in hotels that are served by the free shuttle service that most markets provide. This eliminates parking and traffic hassles and is recommended even if you drive to market. The additional cost of staying in a nearby hotel is usually more than offset by the savings in fuel, parking fees, and wear and tear on you. If you make your reservations early, you can usually find lodging near the center at a reasonable cost.

Establish your buying budget. Several weeks in advance of the show dates, begin establishing your budget for purchases. First estimate the retail value of your current inventory — zero for your first trip. Then estimate sales for the months between the upcoming market and the next one, subtract an allowance for goods purchased locally or through sales representatives, and from these figures calculate the dollar value of goods you should purchase. The easiest way to illustrate is with an example of a buying budget for the July (Christmas) show.

Buying Budget Worksheet – Sample

1. Estimated sales, August through December	$80,000
2. Current inventory retail value	40,000
3. Subtotal (line 1 minus line 2)	40,000
4. Desired retail value of inventory at end of season	30,000
5. Retail value of purchases required (line 3 plus line 4)	70,000
6. Wholesale cost (50% of line 5)	35,000
7. Local and repeat purchases	15,000
8. Budget for market purchases (line 6 minus line 7)	$20,000

A blank Buying Budget Worksheet is provided for your use at the end of this chapter.

Use a worksheet to track purchases. Once you know what your budget is, you should then prepare a Market Buying Worksheet, similar to the illustration below, to help you establish target delivery dates for the total budget. Spread the total amount of your budget into smaller amounts over several months, keeping in mind when your peak sales will occur. A blank Market Buying Worksheet is included at the end of this chapter for you to copy and use when you go to market.

Market Buying Worksheet – Sample

Description of Items Purchased	Budgeted Cost of Goods and Delivery Month				
	Aug. ($3,000)	Sept. ($3,000)	Oct. ($3,000)	Nov. ($7,000)	Dec. ($4,000)
Dayspring		675			
Boyd's Bears	850				
Alice's Cottage				1,254	
Sam's Bowtie			1,098		
Otagiri	295			1,235	
Hill Design		568		2,467	
Lang	875		1,450		
Yankee Candles		650		875	1,450

As each purchase is made, enter the items purchased in the left hand column, and the amount of the purchase under the appropriate column for the delivery date selected, until the amounts are roughly equal to the budget for that month.

Keep running totals of each month as you go. For example, in the Market Buying Worksheet sample, you can see that, so far, $2,020 of the $3,000 budgeted for August has been spent. Obviously, certain seasonal items must be sold in a particular month, so plan your delivery dates carefully. If you have a notebook computer, you can load it with a budget spreadsheet and bring it along. The computer will save you time and be able to give you an instant status report.

For several weeks before attending the market, make lists from magazines and other advertisements of products that attract your interest. Many showrooms and manufacturers send out literature on new products before each show and advertise in the trade magazines. Also use your computer to generate lists of the biggest sellers during the previous year. More information about maintaining your inventory system appears in Chapter 10.

Get to market early. Try to arrive at the market site the afternoon before your first full buying day. Register, collect maps and listings of the vendors and showrooms, and visit a few. However, mostly gather information, and try to get an overall impression of things. If you are a first-time buyer, you could profit by spending a whole day in this endeavor.

Plan to return to your hotel relatively early so you can schedule your activities for the next day. Using the product lists you have accumulated, you can look up manufacturers' locations in the market directory and plan a route that minimizes walking. You will find that you will walk many miles at market, and your feet and back will bear the brunt of fatigue, so it behooves you to plot as straight a course through the booths and showrooms as possible.

Go to the temporary booths first since these are small operators that sometimes tend to take on more orders than they can produce and it is better to get your orders in early. After you have covered your route, then review your purchases, both amounts and kinds, and visit selected booths to fill in the gaps. Plan to spend about three days at a show and leave very tired.

Dress for success and comfort. Perhaps the most important single piece of advice is: Wear comfortable clothes and shoes to market!

While it is not necessary to set style trends at market, you should dress professionally, albeit comfortably. If you dress like a beach bum, you will probably be treated accordingly. A professional appearance will signal the vendors that you are a serious buyer and may strengthen your negotiating position should it become necessary.

Keep all your paperwork organized. Many of the booths offer brochures and price lists that you can collect if you are interested but are not sure you want to carry their merchandise right now. Carry a roomy, but light, briefcase in which to carry them. Accept brochures only if you are truly interested in the wares, or else you will be quickly overloaded with paper, as most vendors will try to get you to take their literature.

As you make purchases, store the invoice copies in a separate compartment in your briefcase, enter the total purchase on the budget sheet, and keep a running total. A pocket calculator is a must! Many vendors don't have time to total your order, and it is easy to lose track of your costs unless you total the invoices.

You should also make sure the invoice identifies the item purchased. This may sound strange, but many vendors use a generic form and enter only codes, not descriptions. After buying several thousand dollars worth of products, it is impossible to remember what each invoice covered. Always ask the vendor to enter a short description of the merchandise on the invoice. Be sure that unit prices are clearly stated for each item.

Purchase Strategies for Market

As mentioned above, most showrooms represent a number of companies, most of which require minimum purchases. Generally, this minimum is a dollar amount, varying from $50 to several thousand for some product lines. Most minimums will be in the $100 to $300 range. Some companies have a minimum quantity, either instead of or in addition to the dollar amount.

In the gift business, most retailers feel more comfortable ordering small amounts to start with to see how the merchandise will sell. Sometimes a retailer will order only one of an item, but generally, two or three is the least number to buy, since one item tends to get lost in the displays. If you are trying to make a statement, you may have to gamble on a larger number.

While minimum buying is a conservative practice for new stores, it has its disadvantages, too. Under-ordering a popular seller can leave you unable to meet the demands, and the demand may wane by the time you reorder and receive a new supply. This can leave you with a supply of the right goods at the wrong time. If you have a strong feeling about a new item, order a large enough quantity to last until you can reorder.

Most companies will require you to prepay your first order or accept it cash on delivery (COD) — COD payments include, not only the costs of goods and shipping costs, but an additional fee for processing the transaction. After one or two COD or prepaid shipments, most will extend credit, usually on a "net 30" basis. This means they will ship merchandise, but you must pay the full amount within 30 days of the invoice date.

Once you establish credit with several companies, you should prepare a credit reference sheet, make copies, and take them with you to market. Many companies will grant credit on your first order if you have several credit references from familiar companies. Others will always require COD on the first order. Still others will never extend credit, although this is the exception.

You will find that virtually all companies pass along the freight charges to you — typically 5 to 15 percent depending on weight, bulk, and distance. This is something important to consider when buying an item that weighs a lot. The wholesale price may sound great, but when you have to figure in the cost of shipping, it runs up the retail price considerably.

Some companies will pay freight on prepaid orders, and others offer special discounts on promotions and specials. It never hurts to ask for information on any special terms.

You should visit the markets and place your orders in plenty of time to receive them before your opening. Place your orders at least two or three months in advance, or further if your opening is near the peak Christmas selling season, when orders are slower in arriving. If you have the sales representative mark the order "New Store Opening," the manufacturer will generally try to make sure the merchandise arrives by a designated date.

The first visit to your store will leave a lasting impression on your customers, so you will want to ensure that you have enough stock to prompt them to come back. From your own experiences, you probably know that a skimpy-looking retail shop does not draw you back as easily as a well-stocked shop does.

We bought a lot of baskets on our first trip to the market because they filled up space and were pretty cheap. Although we survived, probably because of dumb luck, we are convinced we would have grown faster if we had fuller shelves when we opened.

Other Sources for Merchandise

Although you are probably wise to stick to established markets for your initial inventory, don't overlook opportunities for adventure and unusual buying opportunities after you are in stable operation. Take time to follow some adventurous trails, smell the roses, and check the shops. After all, you are getting into this business to have some fun, as well as make money, and you should take some opportunities to enjoy your independence, and perhaps reap some financial benefits, at the same time.

I have the typical male characteristic of zooming down the highway, looking neither to the right nor left, in my determination to get where we are going as soon as possible (even when there is no real reason).

Susie is constantly searching the roadside and signs for opportunities to stop, shop, or just generally explore. So, on our trips, we have this constant battle of wills about getting off the beaten path. However, when we do agree to have an "adventure," it often produces, not only an enjoyable time, but unique merchandise that we otherwise would not have found.

I still would never stop and ask directions, however. There are some portions of the guy code I just will not break!

On a recent trip to Atlanta, we stopped at a rather uninteresting looking craft supply shop, only to find some very well-made furniture displayed. On inquiry, we discovered that the furniture was made in a remote small town even further off the route. After our usual struggle, and the usual result (Susie won!), off we went to the factory, purchased a van load of the furniture (at a good price), and we were back on the road, without any serious time lost.

On another recent trip to the Midwest, we took a very interesting side trip to the Amish country of eastern Pennsylvania. Not only did we experience the awe of spending time in yesteryear, we also found a line of inexpensive pewter jewelry that has been a really good seller for us.

You can also purchase some goods locally, both from individuals and companies. Many local craftspersons make things that you can sell in your shop. These locally made items add a great deal of interest in your product line. They can also help define your store as a source of one-of-a-kind items.

Instead of buying these items outright, take most of them on consignment. This allows you to increase your stock without cost, and you split the sales price with the consignors, accepting a smaller markup, since you do not have your money tied up in the items. The consigning of goods is a bothersome process, however, and requires more recordkeeping, and dealing with more sellers. It also requires you to sometimes turn down items into which people have a personal investment. This can be stressful, especially if the makers are friends or customers. For more suggestions about handling consignments, see Chapter 7.

Finishing Touches

After ordering your initial stock, it is time to turn your attention to finishing and decorating your store. Most lessors will agree to finish out your space two to four weeks before the formal start date of your lease to allow you time to decorate and stock the store before opening day. You should keep up with their progress, and make sure the work gets done on time.

Our first lessor allowed us to come in and decorate before the rent actually started even though he didn't give us any free rent in our lease. This is something you might ask for upfront in your negotiations.

Order Your Sign

You will also need to order your outdoor sign, do your special decorating, have carpet and tile installed, and move in your fixtures. Some of this work can be done concurrently with the lessor's work if you coordinate with the lessor's contractors. Be sure to check with your lessor before you proceed since many of them have very strict requirements as to what you are allowed to do. For example, most shopping centers have very rigid specifications for outdoor signs and window displays in order to control the appearance of their property. Interior decorating is discussed further in Chapter 6.

Train Your Staff

If your business requires employees other than yourself or your partner, recruit and train them for opening day. If you can do without employees at first, you will avoid the hassle of payroll taxes right away, and it allows you, as owners, to learn all aspects of your business before having to train employees.

In our case, we did not hire employees until well after our opening, preferring to handle the chores ourselves.

Advertise Your Grand Opening

You will also want to do some advertising for your opening day. A good idea is to get your regular sign up as soon as possible so people can anticipate and watch the progress. Business and neighborhood sections of local newspapers may feature your shop if they know about your opening. Call your local newspaper's business editor and ask about the possibility of the paper writing a feature article about your new business and its grand opening. Your chances of having an article written about your shop are increased further if you submit a news release before making the call to the business editor.

In addition to contacting the editorial side of your local newspaper, contact its advertising department and request information on ad rates. Consider running ads announcing and promoting your grand opening.

In addition, if your local laws permit, rent a portable sign announcing your opening, and put it out three or four weeks in advance. Consider buying local radio and TV media time to run commercials a day or two before and after your opening day.

To help you with this, locate a small advertising agency. Good agencies will plan a campaign within your budget and help you get the most for your money. Their fees typically come from the media, not you, so it really does not cost any more. They also generally know about advertising specials that you may not be aware of.

Lastly, you may wish to advertise that you will be serving refreshments or giving away small gifts during opening week. A drawing for free merchandise can also create interest in your new store.

Success Strategies

This stage of the business, where you are getting all the details taken care of, can be one of the most stressful times. You will need to finalize a number of issues, such as naming your business, registering with all the appropriate government officials, and getting your merchandise lined up for delivery. Your best survival tactic is to get organized, even if you have never been organized before in your life. Now is the time to:

→ Begin writing notes to yourself, so that you don't have to remember all the details of a conversation or thought.

→ Keep detailed "to do" lists, with checkboxes for when a task is completed.

→ Use a datebook, entering all appointments and checking it every morning, or more frequently.

→ Use the worksheets at the end of this chapter to keep your market purchases on target.

Well, are you ready for the big day? Hopefully, you will be and you will survive it! The next chapter gives some tips on displaying your goods.

Buying Budget Worksheet – Instructions

Fill in the season — such as Christmas, spring, or summer — for which you will be buying merchandise.

1. Estimate your sales for the entire period between the date of the market you are budgeting for and the end of the selling season. If you will go to market in July for the Christmas season, your estimate should cover from August through December. Enter the months in the blanks provided and the amount of your estimate in the far right column.

2. Enter the retail value of the inventory you have on hand.

3. Subtract line 2 from line 1.

4. Enter the retail value of the amount of inventory you would like to have at the end of the season.

5. Add lines 3 and 4 and enter that amount to determine the retail value of the purchases you need to make.

6. Divide line 5 by 2 to determine your wholesale cost of the merchandise.

7. Enter the amount of purchases you will make locally or from other sources, such as repeat purchases of products you already carry.

8. Subtract line 7 from line 6. The result is the amount you should spend at the market. Use the Market Buying Worksheet on page 71 to keep track of your purchases at market.

Buying Budget Worksheet for _____ Season

1. Estimated sales, _____ through _____ $_____

2. Current inventory retail value $_____

3. Subtotal (line 1 minus line 2) $_____

4. Desired retail value of inventory at end of season $_____

5. Retail value of purchases required (line 3 plus line 4) $_____

6. Wholesale cost (50% of line 5) $_____

7. Local and repeat purchases $_____

8. Budget for market purchases (line 6 minus line 7) $_____

Market Buying Worksheet – Instructions

Make several copies of the worksheet. Then enter the date of the market and the selling season for which you are stocking merchandise.

On the first line under the heading, "Budgeted Cost of Goods and Delivery Month," enter the months, included in the selling season, across the page. See the sample in the chapter. Below each month, put in your budgeted amount for that month, according to the seasonality of the merchandise and your projected cash flow. The sum of the amounts under each month should equal the total (line 8) from your Buying Budget Worksheet on page 69.

As you make purchases at market, enter the items in the lefthand column and the costs under the month during which the merchandise is to arrive. Keep a running total of each column so that you don't exceed any month's budget. Remember that you want to plan the arrival of seasonal merchandise appropriately.

Market Buying Worksheet for _____ Season

Market Date: _____

Description of Items Purchased	Budgeted Cost of Goods and Delivery Month				
	$_____	$_____	$_____	$_____	$_____

Chapter 6

Displaying
Your Wares

Display Strategies

Appearance is so important in a retail shop that a great deal of thought needs to go into the planning and execution of your displays. Master chefs are taught the importance of presentation of food. It is not enough that food be delicious and nourishing; it must also be appealing to the eye. That is why parsley growers survive. Not many people eat it, but tons are used as decoration on platters of fish and other foods. Why? Parsley provides a touch of color on an otherwise drab plate, which makes you want to order it.

Some restaurants feature color photographs of their specialties, displayed around their dining rooms. They are invariably colorful, balanced displays of their food that invite you to partake. Unfortunately, the real food doesn't always match the photos. But the point is that it is not enough to have useful, quality merchandise, you must display it in a way that invites the customer to take it home. Although attracted to an item, your customers often don't know how they can use it. Your display can show how.

Be Distinctive

Imagination is the key ingredient to planning eye-catching and appealing displays. Don't be afraid to do something different, maybe even a little outlandish at times, within the bounds of good taste, of course. The more distinctive your store, the more your customers will remember it.

Even if you are part of a franchise, it is a good idea to add your own special touches to set your store apart from the cookie cutter, stamped-out look of many franchises. For instance, card shops tend to look alike, so the ones that use some imagination really stand out in their customers' memories. You may even have noticed that some McDonald's restaurants have been decorated so as to add creative touches that set them apart. For example, one that is particularly attractive has a nostalgia theme, using antique toys, old pictures, and other memorabilia to achieve a very warm atmosphere in a normally cold and sterile fast food serving area.

Susie is the unquestioned czar of displays in our stores. One craftsperson tried to talk her into handling a line of Doggie Caskets in our gift shop. While that would have been distinctive, and would have been remembered by customers, she doubted that they would have been motivated to return.

Decide on a Look

Your next step is deciding on a look. This can go in many directions from whimsical to very formal, with anything in between. Your direction will be determined mainly by the products you want to sell and the customers you are trying to attract.

Have you ever been in shops that really turned you off and made you not want to go back? Naturally, you want yours to have the opposite effect, and you want the look to be as distinctively yours as possible.

You don't have to settle for an unwelcoming interior decor just because the space you are leasing is plain, box-shaped, and finished in a generic and boring standard decor. Not many people are attracted to a shop that looks like a warehouse bay, unless, perhaps, you are selling industrial chemicals and forklifts. With a little imagination, you can transform "plain vanilla" into a "hot fudge sundae!" When you look at a rental space, train yourself to see beyond the obvious to the possibilities.

For example, suppose you are opening a country shop, and you are not able to find an old house in a good location. You can achieve the atmosphere you want by using wallpaper, wood trim, and antiques to give a homey atmosphere to a plain, vanilla-box space in a strip center. Sectioning off the large space into small, room-sized spaces can give a warmer feel to it. Try using furniture to accomplish this effect, or lace curtains in the windows and rolling flower boxes set outside each morning to give it a cottage effect. To take it even further, reduce the number of commercial fluorescent light fixtures and add ceiling fans with schoolhouse light fixtures, spaced throughout your shop to enhance the homey look. If you also sell lamps, they can be used for supplemental lighting in the room-sized spaces.

We built a unique checkout counter with a gazebo-like canopy that gives the effect of a cottage within the space. This is positioned near the front of the store, in the center, to serve as a central focal point to customers entering the shop. In our second store, we used the room-division technique, accented by false wooden beams between the dividers. We also salvaged some weathered boards from an old fence at our residence and applied them to the rear wall to achieve a lap-siding effect. We have received many positive comments on the effects we have achieved using these rather simple and inexpensive decorating techniques.

All this is to say that you can make a silk purse out of a sow's ear if the desire is there. You can do just about anything if you put your imagination to work. Consider this story about a woman who has a gift shop in a service station. The gas pumps are still bringing in a major portion of her income, but she has added a beautiful gift shop, carrying everything from small gift items to expensive collectibles. She enjoys seeing the faces of her customers when they walk in to pay for their gas and are surprised to find that this is not your usual gas station!

Research Display Ideas

A good way to get display ideas is to look around when visiting other retail shops. Go to other towns and look at shops similar to yours. You may not want to copy their ideas exactly, but it may trigger a new idea for you. See what appeals to you and make a note of it. Likewise, note things you don't like, so you won't make the same mistake. Does this approach sound familiar? It should, because this is the way most people decorate their homes; looking around, filing away good ideas, and discarding ideas they don't like. Your shop may not be able to mirror your home decorating scheme, but it can reflect your tastes. This can be your chance to be a little bolder than you would at home.

You can also find some pretty good ideas by going to trade shows and noticing the displays of the vendors. Some are really professional, while some obviously did not put much thought into displaying their wares. Trade magazines are also good research sources, or just magazines, in general.

You may want to hire professional help for your displays. Some franchises offer this service, and some may insist on certain forms of display. But even large card companies give the owners some leeway to inject their own personalities into the atmosphere of their shop. Whether or not you get professional help may depend on your feeling of self-confidence in this area — or it may depend more on your financial situation. If you have decided to take this big plunge into retail, you probably have some pretty good ideas, so go with them.

Decide on Permanent Versus Moveable Displays

After you have decided on a look and done some research, it is time to think about permanent and moveable displays. You may not want any permanent displays — this is entirely up to you. This decision will probably depend on the type of merchandise you wish to sell. Moveable fixtures are more flexible and keep the shop from becoming boring by looking the same all of the time. This is important in gift, decorating, furniture, and other shops that depend upon creating an ambience to put customers in a buying mood, and in shops that depend on illustrating ideas for using their products. If you are selling hardware, paint, or garden tools, this is obviously not a critical consideration.

If your product line is for indoor use, you can use furniture for a good portion of your displays. The furniture can even be for sale, but sometimes, when a display piece is so covered up with merchandise, the customer may not realize it is for sale. Be aware also that using furniture for display over a long period may damage it, thus reducing its resale value.

We have not been super successful in selling our furniture, and we suspect it is because our shop is so full that it is hard for potential buyers to focus on the furniture. We are experimenting with setting up a separate furniture-only area, with only enough accessories around to accentuate the furniture. We will have to see if the increased furniture sales compensate for the loss of the display space for our gift items and accessories, especially since we carry only a limited number of pine reproduction pieces, not a complete furniture line.

It is probably a good idea to have a mixture of permanent and moveable displays. This should give you the flexibility that you need. If you need display pieces that you are not able to build, look in your phone book's Yellow Pages under "Store Fixtures" for companies that specialize in fixtures of all kinds, both new and used. You may also be able to find local cabinetmakers or craftspeople to custom build the items that you need. Other useful sources include garage sales, flea markets, and auctions.

One advantage of a country shop is being able to pick up old, primitive items that can be used to enhance your look. In these times of nostalgia, these pieces will fit in with many different themes.

One of our favorite finds was some old kitchen cabinets that were in terrible shape, with paint peeling and nail holes. We scraped most of the old paint off and repainted them. We use them to display our gourmet and country food lines, and they have been a source of many compliments from customers.

We finished the country kitchen look by building primitive base cabinets with old feed sack curtains instead of doors, fitted with an old sink and water faucet. The whole display cost less than fifty dollars, proving that you can be creative and frugal at the same time. We know we have achieved the homey look we are seeking when customers tell us they would like to live in our shop.

Keep Your Displays Fresh

You must constantly find new ways to display. You can't let your displays become stagnant. You must constantly update and change them to keep customer interest. One successful trick is to move things around every once in a while.

Old merchandise moved to a new spot will sometimes make the customer think it is newly arrived. This sounds strange, but it really works. This is especially true when you get a clientele that comes in on a regular basis. Regular customers are one reason to keep adding new merchandise so that you can keep these customers interested. Many customers will come in and simply ask, "What new things have arrived?"

Store Layout Strategies

Now, you are ready to decide on a floor plan. The most efficient method, which is also easier on the back and the nerves, is to make a graph of the floor dimensions, measure the display pieces, cut out paper pieces to their scale, and place them on the graph so that you are able to move them around until you come up with the optimum arrangement. Be sure to keep in mind that you need a smooth-flowing traffic pattern. This should determine where the displays and the check-out counter are placed.

In most instances, it is more attractive to have something set up in the center section along with things against the walls. It is pretty boring to walk into a shop where everything is displayed against the outer walls, plus, you lose a lot of good display area. Be careful not to put breakable items on an unsteady surface where people can bump into it — that is a common-sense rule of display.

When possible, try to match products with displays. For instance, display items such as foods, magnets, spice trivets, and cookbooks, in one area, such as the kitchen cabinet display used by Homespun Cottage.

You can set up similar areas for children's clothes and toys, adult clothing and jewelry, each decorated with a compatible theme. Some highly pilferable items should be located where you can see and control access to them, such as at your checkout counter.

Your checkout counter should be located toward the front of the shop so that you can greet your customers individually as they come in the door. You want to be careful not to appear pushy or put pressure on them to buy, but it is important to be in a position to acknowledge their presence.

Window Displays

Window displays are very important — they need to be made interesting enough to encourage people to come in and see what else you have for them. Some shop owners feel it is important that potential customers cannot see everything in the store from the front window. This strategy makes customers want to explore a little further by coming inside. One expensive mistake you can avoid is that you should not put anything in the window that might fade if your store frontage has exposure to direct sunlight.

The lace curtains we had in the window of our first shop were an amazing drawing card that brought in customers just passing by in their cars. We sold the lace in our shop, so we received double the benefits by attracting people to our shop with a product that was also for sale. If curtains are appropriate to your shop, take time to plan them so they will attract attention from several yards away.

Seasonal Displays

Seasonal displays can be great fun and a tremendous amount of work. Choose the special holidays that will work best for you and concentrate on them. For many businesses, you will want to put the most time and effort into your Christmas decorations.

If you have a special Christmas event, you need to have a date in mind when ordering your Christmas merchandise. This is usually done in July — which is pretty hard to get used to — and you will need to specify a shipping date to ensure arrival in plenty of time.

Not all holidays are good for all businesses, so don't spend much time or money in preparing for them. Concentrate on those times that work well and add others as the need and interest arises.

Your seasonal display can be little more than a table decorated with gifts suitable for that special time or occasion. Set in a highly visible space, this may be sufficient for your shop if you are not heavily into seasonal merchandise.

Our Christmas decorations go up in November, in conjunction with our annual Christmas Open House. After closing, on the night before our open house, we work like little elves — well, maybe not so little — to put up the tree, get out the greenery and all the Christmas merchandise, and generally trim the shop in the holiday spirit. This is a pretty tiring venture, but well worth the effort.

Our best times seem to be Christmas, Valentine's Day, Mother's Day, and the end of school — we sell lots of teachers' gifts.

Success Strategies

Displays call for creative talents that not all personalities possess. Recognizing these differences in abilities, and dividing the work accordingly, will greatly improve display quality, not to mention preserving domestic tranquility in husband-wife partnerships. If no one in your business is creatively inclined, enlist someone with a flair for decorating to assist you with planning and setting up your displays. Some knowledge can be acquired in these areas, through study and seminars, but excellence in display skills comes more from innate ability than learning.

Chapter 7

Setting
House Rules

Establishing Your Operating Policies

A seemingly endless number of questions will arise when you enter the retail business, and as a result, decisions must be made. Among the questions you will face are issues surrounding:

- Pricing policies
- Consignment policies
- Purchasing unsolicited products
- Credit policies
- Cash layaway policies
- Returns
- Special orders
- Damage policies
- Children in the store
- Hours of operation
- Credit cards
- Gift wrapping
- Gift registry

In addition to these basic nuts-and-bolts types of issues, you will also have to reflect on the moral standards of conduct for your business. While the first part of this chapter discusses basic business issues, the last part of this chapter examines some of the questionable gray areas of retail practice that you will want to avoid.

Until you start your business, you will really have no idea just how many decisions you will have to make about the day-to-day operations of the store. Instead of waiting for each situation to arise and then formulating a response — a process that will result in making some mistakes and missing out on some opportunities — take some time before your opening to formulate your operating policies, put them in writing, and supply copies to all your employees. You may also wish to post some of these policies, such as layaway policies and check and credit card acceptance, for your customers. Taking the time to anticipate and formulate responses to common, recurring situations will pay off in better customer relations and more profitable operations. Below are some insights into these areas, in the hope that they will be helpful to you in setting up some house rules.

Pricing Policies

Pricing will be one of the most important decisions you will make since it affects that all-important variable, profit, in a very direct manner. You must strike a delicate balance between a price that is high enough to allow you to achieve a reasonable profit margin and yet low enough to keep your merchandise affordable and competitive. Most retailers use a 50 percent markup, known in the trade as keystone. What this means, in plain language, is doubling your cost to establish the retail price. Since markup is figured on the sales price, this results in what is considered a 50 percent markup in retail terminology. For example, if your cost on an item is $1, your selling price would be $2. Fifty percent of $2 is $1, which is your markup.

Markup terminology was probably developed to avoid using a term that admits to a 100 percent increase. Most consumers would be appalled that you are selling something for double what you paid for it. They would be inclined to ask why you don't carry a gun and wear a mask. Most consumers just haven't had any exposure to the myriad costs involved in running a business, and they are used to thinking in terms of net profit figures that they have heard or seen in the media. A person may read that Sears had sales of $300 million with a net profit of seven percent, and therefore, assume that Sears marks up its goods only seven percent. In actuality, net profit is calculated by subtracting overhead expenses from gross profit, which is total sales minus the costs of the merchandise.

Because of this misconception about pricing on the part of the buying public, don't be surprised that some of your customers think you are Jack the Ripper when they find out about your markup. You will be amazed by the number of people who will offer to sell you their goods for $10, and suggest you can sell them for $12 and make a tidy $2 profit. Nearly everyone thinks the same way before they go into business.

Although it is true that higher volumes will make up for lower prices to some extent, unless you can sell as much as a K Mart or Wal-Mart, you absolutely need at least a 50 percent markup to survive in a small retail shop. Although doubling the price may sound outrageous, it does not result in excessive profits when you consider the expenses you must pay for rent, taxes, insurance, supplies, and labor.

Our net profit margins have been in the 9 to 15 percent range, using a 50 percent markup. Even though we target a 50 percent gross profit — gross sales less the cost of goods — the actual figure runs about 47 percent, because of unrecovered freight costs and the fact that you cannot mark up every item 50 percent because of competition and your market's ability to pay.

Sometimes you will have to sell an item at a lower markup if you feel you cannot compete at full keystone. Be careful, however, not to price too many items this way, or you will find nothing left for yourself at the end of the year. You can try to balance out your gross profit by marking some items up slightly higher to compensate for the lower markups on others. You can do this when you get a special discount, or are able to buy items direct from a manufacturer.

If you aren't going to use the standard 50 percent markup, the following is a quick way to calculate your selling price.

$$\text{Selling price} = \frac{\text{Cost of item}}{100 - (\text{Markup percentage})} \times 100$$

For example, assume an item costs you $10, and you want to use a markup of 35 percent. The selling price would then be calculated as:

$$\text{Selling price} = \frac{10.00}{100 - 35} \times 100 \quad \text{or} \quad \frac{10.00}{65} \times 100 = \$15.38$$

Do not multiply the cost by 35 percent and add that amount back to the cost. That will produce a retail markup of 17.5 percent, not 35 percent.

One area where pricing policy must remain flexible, and where you can frequently achieve much greater markups, is in collectibles and limited editions. If you have a hot collectible item, its market value will increase markedly as it goes out of production or print, and you will be able to take advantage of the increased demand in your pricing policies.

Examples of items that frequently increase in value are limited edition prints, dolls, figurines, and antiques of all kinds. A word of caution, here — resist the temptation to exact outrageous prices just because you have a scarcity. This may gain some short-term profits at the expense of long-term customer patronage.

> *We rarely increase a price because a product is in short supply, and then only modestly to help compensate for reduced markups on other items.*

Your customers will appreciate the fact that you keep your prices fair, when other stores are jacking up prices on hard-to-get items. This strategy will repeatedly pay off in customer loyalty and increased sales. No one likes to feel they are being ripped off.

Don't overlook freight in your cost of merchandise. If your competition will allow, add the freight to the cost before you apply the markup. Most of the time, however, you will simply have to add freight to the marked up price, thus recovering only the cost of the freight.

Consignment Policies

Consignment is the practice of allowing sellers to place merchandise in your store for sale, with payment to be made only after the sale is made. You need to set up careful records to keep track of consignment sales. Before accepting merchandise, prepare a written agreement for each consignor to sign that states when payments will be made, who is responsible for loss or damage, and how long an item is allowed to stay without selling. This written agreement can eliminate misunderstandings later.

One advantage to consignment is that consignors are also potential customers, who will come in frequently to check on their merchandise and are likely to make purchases during these visits.

This policy can also be a disadvantage since some consignors, in their understandable zeal to have their products sell, may want to control the display and placement of their goods in your store. For example, a consignor may become incensed that an item is not being given the prominence he or she believes it deserves, and remove it from the store. Don't allow the lower profit consignment items to push your own merchandise off the shelves! It is important to retain control over your displays, and written agreements with consignors can reduce friction in this area.

We take only a few consignment items, and mainly because our customers like the idea of buying locally made crafts. Because we do not pay for these items until they sell, we use a markup of only 35 percent on these items.

In our consignment agreement, we stipulate that we will pay our consignors on the tenth of each month following the sale and generally assume liability for losses. We require the items to be removed when we request it. If an item has not sold in two to three months, we usually ask the consignor to pick it up.

Purchasing Unsolicited Products

You will frequently be besieged by individuals or peddlers trying to sell you their wares directly, during your shop hours. While some good quality merchandise can be bought this way, be careful about buying off trucks and out of the trunks of cars. There is some possibility that you are being offered stolen merchandise, or very bad seconds, which you may not recognize until the peddler is long gone.

In addition, dealing with every peddler — or recognized sales representative, for that matter — can interfere with serving your customers, and you should not hesitate to tell vendors you do not have time to purchase goods during selling hours. Suggest they make an appointment to return when you have help or on a slack day. They can be persistent, but reputable sellers will be happy to accommodate your needs and desires. Telephone solicitors are among the most bothersome interruptions to your business day. Learn how to say "no" and hang up the phone promptly.

Credit Policies

The summary advice on credit is short and sweet — don't do it. As a new business owner, you have too many problems without having to deal with accounts receivable. Most people don't expect to receive credit in a small shop and will not be offended, particularly if you accept credit cards and offer layaways.

Cash Layaway Policies

Layaways are a good substitute for credit, and without the risks. Decide in advance the dollar amounts and period of time you will allow for using layaways. For example, you might allow layaways for articles that cost more than $20 and for a period of 90 days. Once the stated policy is in place, you do not necessarily have to rigidly enforce these limits, and you can work with regular customers within reasonable limits.

You will want to buy layaway tags from your office supply store and use them to track these items. The best tag to use is a three-part tag, with one copy given to the customer, one placed in a file box, and the other attached to the item in storage.

Keep in mind that layaways do require more storage space, especially just before Christmas and other holidays. Set aside a special section in your storage room, and place layaway items on shelves, indexed by the tag numbers.

Returns

As soon as you open for business, you will hear the inevitable question: "Can I bring this back if . . .?" A customer's reasons for possibly returning merchandise might be:

- It doesn't fit.
- It doesn't look good in my house.
- It makes my spouse angry.
- It isn't what the person wanted.

You should be prepared with your answer beforehand. Your policy on returns will obviously depend, to some degree, on what you sell. Health laws and hygiene considerations, for example, would preclude you from accepting returns of intimate garments after being worn. Opened foodstuffs, software, books, and similar items that can spoil or be copied present similar problems.

In these days, when superior customer service may be the only thing that allows you to compete with the big stores, you should try to be as liberal as possible on returns. It may be to your advantage to accept a few unreasonable returns, since such actions often inspire customer loyalty that will produce greater sales over the long haul.

Customers who feel they have been treated well on returns often tell their friends, thus producing invaluable word-of-mouth advertising. Problems experienced as a result of giving this form of good customer service will almost always be overwhelmingly exceeded by the increased goodwill your store will enjoy.

But, you do need to set some boundaries. Some customers will push the envelope on returns and take advantage to the point of damaging your business. For example, some will want to return seasonal merchandise after the season is over, when you will not be able to resell the items. Others will attempt to return sale merchandise for a full refund. You would do well to consider a return policy with the following elements:

• All merchandise returned in good condition will be accepted except sale merchandise and collectibles or other unique items whose value is decreased or destroyed by opening or use. Be sure to post notices during sales that all sales on these items are final.

• Seasonal merchandise returned after the season will receive store credit only, not a cash refund.

• Merchandise returned after 30 days will receive store credit only.

A good idea is to post your return policy or include it on your sales slips if you have them customized. Otherwise, be sure your employees are aware of your policy and can explain it if asked. It is also a good idea to retain some flexibility to accommodate individual cases. You can authorize employees to use their judgment to grant exceptions, or have them refer these cases to you for a decision. Remember that a liberal return policy makes customers feel comfortable dealing with you.

Special Orders

Special orders are another matter that you should consider when you set up your rules for operation. They can represent a significant source of income since customers are often willing to pay a premium price to pick out a specific color or style of goods that they need. You should try to accommodate most special orders, and even keep samples of some items for that purpose.

There are pitfalls, however. Be sure to get a significant down payment for special orders — usually half the retail price — before you place the order. Otherwise, you can end up being stuck with unique merchandise when customers change their minds, move away, or simply disappear. Be careful also about special ordering an item for a customer when you must order a large minimum quantity. If the product is a slow seller, you may wind up with a large quantity of duds in order to make one small sale.

> We carry lace curtains that we can only purchase by the half-bolt — about 15 yards. Therefore, we are reluctant to special order two or three yards unless we are confident the rest of the bolt will sell.

Damage Policies

You have probably seen signs in stores that say, "Lovely to look at delightful to hold. If you break it, we mark it sold," or something equally cutesy. While this may give some shop owners some satisfaction, such attitudes and policies actually cost money through ill will and consequent reduced patronage and sales. Your best course of action is to simply grit your teeth, smile, and graciously accept your loss when a customer or a child breaks something in your store.

Children in the Store

Speaking of damage, Rambo himself cannot inflict as much destruction to your merchandise as a determined three- or four-year-old, whose mother or father doesn't seem to notice or care that he or she is bent on wasting your premises. While you still don't want to impose damages on the little tykes or their parents, you can take steps to minimize the carnage.

First, provide child-size tables and chairs, along with coloring books, crayons, and children's books to keep the little darlings occupied. Furthermore, make sure you suggest this activity to parents when they first enter the store. If a child is simply running wild, politely suggest that the child may get hurt and hope the parent will get the hint.

If not, try to move stuff out of reach, and pray that the parent remembers that roast in the oven and leaves.

People are more easily offended over their children than almost anything else, so use extreme caution and your best diplomacy in dealing with these situations.

Hours of Operation

You should set and post conspicuously your hours of operation. These will vary depending on your location, hours of neighboring stores, your community customs, and your lessor's rules. Try keeping track of sales versus time of day for several months and adjust your hours accordingly. If you are the only employee, give due consideration to human endurance. Don't try to push yourself beyond your limits or you will be faced with illness brought on by fatigue, and it may cost you more to pay substitutes, if you can get them, than reducing your work hours.

Whatever hours you post, it is important that you adhere to them. Customers will stop coming to your store if they can't rely on you being open during posted hours.

Credit Cards

You may as well resign yourself to accepting major credit cards. While it costs you to process them, the American consumer has come to rely on them, and you will miss out on too many sales if you don't take them.

We accept Mastercard, Visa, American Express, and Discover, although we added the last two more recently as more and more customers wanted to use them. We started out using a manual imprinter, which was adequate for the first couple of years. As sales increased and technology developed, we went to a terminal in each store. The terminal instantly reads the card, issues the receipt, and credits our bank account.

Because of advancing technology, convenience, and availability, in this day and age you will want to start out with a credit card terminal and accept at least all of the cards mentioned above. Generally, you will use a lease-purchase plan to get a credit card terminal. However, this cost is at least partially offset by the discount rate — the fee charged for processing — charged by the credit card companies, which is lower than for the hand-processed charge slips. They also are much faster, and do not require telephone authorization for large purchases, as the manual charges do.

Shop around for the best rate — usually two to four percent — and a bank or organization that takes most cards. Be aware that some banks have fairly high charges for processing the card charges and do not accept all cards. Other services take more cards, charge lower fees, and have better systems for processing the paperwork and handling the approval process.

Ask your bank for the names of some companies that process credit cards, and shop around for the package that best fits your needs at the lowest cost. As mentioned earlier, most of these processing companies will furnish the terminals for a monthly rental or under a monthly payment plan that allows you to eventually own them outright.

Some credit cards are more prevalent in particular locations, and you will be wise to accommodate the prevailing plastic of your customers. For example, American Express has traditionally been the card of choice for business travelers and upper income consumers, although that is changing somewhat with the increasing popularity of Visa and Mastercard, especially the Gold Card versions.

If you are in a resort or convention location, however, you will be wise to include American Express and Diners Club cards in your list of accepted cards. This is also recommended if you cater to a high income group.

Gift Wrapping

Having a gift wrapping service or not is another decision you may need to make. If you operate a gift shop, it is almost a necessity to provide some form of packaging for gifts. You will find that the costs of attractive wrapping paper, boxes, ribbons, and gift bags are significant, and that wrapping requires a certain amount of skill to produce an attractive package.

If you possess the skills, you will then need to decide whether or not to charge for the service. While most customers are willing to pay, you may opt to provide it as a service rather than charging. In order to minimize costs, you can use kraft gift bags, on which you could place your shop logo and name via an attractive sticker. The bags can then be decorated with colored tissue and ribbons or attractive ties.

Gift Registry

You should also consider offering a gift registry, so that brides and others can select merchandise they like for purchase by friends and family. Other customers will also use this service to help spouses and family with Christmas and other special occasion shopping. Your registry can be as simple as keeping a looseleaf notebook, with pages filed alphabetically for each registrant, listing his or her choices. When an item is purchased, mark it off in the book.

Business Ethics

A final area that needs some discussion is the topic of business ethics. While most people are moral individuals and want to do the right thing, you need to make some conscious decisions about your business practices in some gray areas. Few merchants would deliberately cheat customers, file false tax returns, or commit other offenses that can be classified as black or white. Gray areas, however, occur frequently, and it will be up to you to establish standards of conduct for your business that reflect your moral principles.

This discussion becomes timely as our national government continues to suffer a loss of confidence because of real and alleged ethical violations, evidenced nightly on the evening news. Recent newspaper articles and television news stories have also reported a growing resistance from consumers to what they perceive as unethical business practices. You do not want your business to suffer from the same loss of confidence as government. Therefore, it pays to establish policies that are just and ethical and ensure fair treatment of your most valuable asset, your customers.

Questionable Practices

What consumers perceive as being unethical may not always be the case. As mentioned previously, some customers, because of their unfamiliarity with the costs you must recover, will consider it unethical if you mark up your merchandise by more than a few percent. Most of them, however, when the situation is explained, will recognize and grant you the right to a fair return on your money and labor. You should never be ashamed of setting policies that ensure this.

Even if you are inclined to make exorbitant profits, competition will generally prevent it. Obviously, the concept of fair return will vary from individual to individual, and cannot be defined precisely, but do not consider a net profit in the 10 to 20 percent range to be excessive, given the risks and the investment you have in your retail business. In the final analysis, however, you must decide for yourself what is a fair profit. Some other practices that are questionable from an ethical standpoint are described below.

Continuous sale prices. You probably know of shops where all or most of the merchandise carries tags announcing each item as "usually" sold at a higher price, but "now" offered at a lower price. These tags never seem to change, so you have good reason to question the reality of the "sale" price. Then, when you ask if you can order more at the reduced price, you are told yes, giving further credence to the suspicion that it is not a sale at all. Instead you suspect the item is being marked up artificially to mislead you, the customer, into believing that you are getting a bargain. You do not want to do this!

When you mark something down, take a percentage off from your original intended price so that it really represents a savings to the buyer. Your customers will come to understand this, and then you will generally have no trouble selling an item at a reduced price. Of course, you will end up with a few "dogs" that you can't unload at any price, and you will wonder if you were sane when you bought them! But, that is the exception, not the rule.

You should strive towards having only two or three sales a year, and these sales should last for only a limited time — one to three weeks, normally. If your customers realize that you have continuous or frequent sales, you will have a difficult time selling anything at regular price. Then, either you won't be around long, or you will have to resort to deceptive markups.

Advertising extremely low prices on very limited stock. Some retailers will advertise an item for sale at a very low price, but only have one or two to sell. Customers resent being sucked in on a ruse. If you can, do not advertise prices; instead, base the appeal of your shop on its service, its uniqueness, and the attractiveness of your merchandise. If you must depend on price as a major feature, be truthful and have ample supplies of sale items.

Sensational or misleading advertising. How many fake telegrams have you received from recreational resorts that promise you have won either a new car, a house in the country, or a fishing boat, only to find out, if you actually visit the place, that you have won a $50 inflatable raft? Most people won't believe these kinds of wild claims and will be turned off by them.

Overall, the best policy to follow is one that gives you a fair return, gives the customer solid value for his or her dollar, and treats the customer as a rational adult. While there may be some who like being fooled, most just want to deal in good faith with a merchant they can trust, and you will be well-served to cater to this larger group. Those are the rules under which most retailers try to operate.

Dealing with Other's Ethics

On the other side of the ethics coin, you will find that there are unethical customers and vendors with whom you will have to deal. Although it is tempting to retaliate in kind, resist it. Consider this story about a businessperson who purchased a newspaper from the newsstand owner in his building each day, always greeting the man with a cheerful "Good Morning" even though the greeting was never returned. When a friend asked why he persisted with his greetings when they were never reciprocated, the businessperson replied that he never allowed someone else to control his actions or attitudes. Accordingly, never let unethical conduct of others cause you to sacrifice your principles.

Success Strategies

By thinking about the rules and limits you set for your customers and yourself in advance of opening your store, you will be able to enforce your rules with confidence. Your ease and self-confidence will inspire those who deal with you to have trust, faith, and respect for your decisions.

Furthermore, you can't beat that old retailing axiom that the customer is always right. And, although it may require exerting considerable restraint and self-control, your business will be better off if you observe it.

Always consider any problem from your customer's viewpoint. You know how you like to be treated as a customer, so you can always fall back on this golden rule when you are faced with a perplexing problem. Besides, the vast majority of customers are honest, considerate citizens who are just as anxious to get along as you are, and they make it all worthwhile!

❖ Part III ❖

Retail Business Management

Chapter 8

Managing Your Cash

Handling Daily Receipts

Instead of being about sophisticated techniques for maximizing your return on invested funds, this chapter deals with those mundane, often trivial details associated with the daily process of exchanging the merchandise in your store for currency, checks, and credit card slips. Other, much better, sources for advice are available on the weightier financial matters involved in business management, which are discussed further in Chapter 9.

Some suggestions on specific procedures for handling your daily receipts and making payments are covered in this chapter.

Managing the Cash Drawer

In your retail business, you can expect to receive payment in one of four forms. This section describes the details for handling each of these four types of transactions.

- Cash
- Checks
- Credit cards
- Travelers checks

Cash. Probably the first questions you will need to answer are: how much cash should you keep in your store for change and how should you replenish it each day? If most of your items sell for less than $40, you can probably start out with $125 in your cash drawer. Ideally, this amount is approximately broken down into the following denominations.

Cash Drawer Setup

Denomination	Amount	Denomination	Amount
quarters	$5.00	one-dollar bills	$20.00
dimes	3.00	five-dollar bills	75.00
nickels	1.50	ten-dollar bills	20.00
pennies	0.50		

Of course, your first cash drawer will look slightly different in its breakdown since rolls of coins from the bank come in larger quantities than the quarters, dimes, and nickels above. The main idea is to maintain an adequate supply for making change. You replenish your cash each time you make a bank deposit, although you will not exactly restore the same distribution among the various bill and coin denominations. Simply monitor each denomination, and replenish each when it gets too low.

Whether or not you accept personal checks will affect the amounts and denominations you keep in your cash drawer. If you accept personal checks, you will probably find that 50 to 75 percent of your receipts are checks. If you do not accept checks, or if you sell merchandise in a different price range, you may need to adjust your cash drawer contents accordingly.

If most of your merchandise sells for less than five or ten dollars and you do not accept checks, you can probably get by with a lower total amount, although you will probably need more coins and one-dollar bills. If you carry very expensive merchandise, it will almost be a necessity to accept checks and credit cards, and this will probably reduce your change requirements. If possible, check with a similar store in another area for their experience.

Making change for customers is one area where many mistakes can occur. Train yourself and your employees how to correctly count change back to customers, even if you have a modern cash register that calculates the change for you. For example, if the purchase comes to $3.70 and the customer pays with a five-dollar bill, you would select a nickel, a quarter, and a one-dollar bill from the drawer. Then, beginning with the smallest denomination, you would hand the money to the customer while counting up from $3.70, saying: "$3.75" as you hand over the nickel; "$4.00" as you give the quarter; and "$1.00 makes five" as you lay the dollar bill down.

Experienced cashiers always leave the customer's payment out until the change is counted back since customers often forget whether they paid with a five-, ten-, or twenty-dollar bill. Having the bill to show them clears up any confusion and saves you and your customer from any embarrassing scenes.

Checks. You will need to decide what your policy on check acceptance will be. If your business deals mainly with a local clientele, you can probably implement a rather liberal check acceptance policy, only requiring that current addresses and phone numbers be printed on the checks. With the right types of customers to whom you sell your products — and some plain good luck — you will most likely experience few losses, in spite of the numerous horror stories you have heard about bounced checks.

When we started our business, we had heard so many horror stories of bouncing checks that we implemented our rather liberal check acceptance policy with some trepidation. However, after more than eight years of operation, we are still amazed that we have experienced hardly any losses due to bad checks. We have had checks returned, but, so far — knock on wood — we have been able to collect virtually all of them ourselves, with occasional assistance from our bank.

If you will be selling mainly to tourists or to a customer group with known credit problems, or if your area of operations has a history of bad checks, you should consider signing up with one of the check verification and insuring agencies that operate all over the country. Your bank can refer you to some reliable companies. Other precautions you can take are:

↪ Require an ID or driver's license number. This way you can check that the address on the check is current, which will allow you to contact the customer in the event of a problem.

↪ Call the bank to verify that funds are sufficient if the check is for a large amount and you don't know the customer.

↪ Make sure the check is signed and the amount is correct.

↪ Deposit checks promptly.

Credit cards. Credit cards must be accepted in accordance with your bank or agency's rules. If you do not have an electronic terminal, most card companies require verification by telephone of amounts that exceed a given amount, with the limit set anywhere from $50 to $150. During the call, you will be given an authorization number. You should always check the expiration date of the card, and check the signature against another ID if you have any doubts.

Travelers checks. Travelers checks are simple, and the only requirement is that the checks be signed in your presence. They are treated as any other check.

Reconciling Daily Receipts and Sales

The next questions are how to reconcile your daily receipts and sales and prepare your bank deposits. In addition to the cash that you take in from sales, you must also take into account any cash disbursements you make from the cash drawer. While you should make most purchases by check, it is almost impossible to avoid paying for some minor items from your cash if you do not keep a separate petty cash account. Each cash payment is recorded daily on cash disbursement slips and later entered on the books, right along with any checks written, as will be discussed in Chapter 9.

Reconciling your daily receipts is a very simple process that only takes a few minutes each day. You will generally need to reconcile the following on a daily basis:

• Cash received

• Checks received

• Charge card slips received

• Minor cash disbursements

All of these will need to be balanced against your sales tickets. For sales tickets, you can use the cheapest two-part sales books money can buy. Enter each sale on a ticket, listing your inventory code, price per item, extended sales amount, sales tax, and the total due. Give one copy to the customer and retain the other one for your records. You can customize these tickets by using a rubber stamp to place your store name and address on the customers' copies during slack period.

At the end of the day, the easiest way to start is by counting up your cash drawer and restoring it to your permanent change amount. To do this, start counting the pennies, then nickels, dimes, and quarters into even increments approximating the ideal denominations shown earlier in this chapter. Odd change amounts will go into your bank deposit. Then count one-, five-, and ten-dollar bills until you reach your permanent change amount, for example $125.

Once you have the drawer ready for the next day, set it aside. Next, you simply total all sales from the tickets, cash taken from the drawer exceeding your change, checks, credit card slips, and cash disbursements. Then, you can use a simple reconciliation sheet, such as the one at the end of this chapter or one you make yourself, set up with columns as follows:

Daily Reconciliation Worksheet Setup

Column 1 – Date

Column 2 – Sales slips totals

Column 3 – Cash from drawer (after setting aside permanent cash drawer amount for change)

Column 4 – Cash disbursement slip totals

Column 5 – Adjusted cash = (column 3 + column 4)

Column 6 – Total checks

Column 7 – Total credit card slips

Column 8 – Balance* (sum of columns 5, 6, and 7 minus column 2)

Column 9 – Total deposit** (columns 3, 6, and 7)

* This should be zero if no errors are made, or it will indicate the amount you are over or under for the day.

** If you use a credit card terminal, only columns 3 and 6 will be included in your bank deposit, since the electronic terminal automatically makes deposits to your bank.

The daily reconciliation will help you determine the amount of your bank deposit and whether the day's cash transactions have been handled accurately.

If you are out of balance and cannot find the error, you should fill out a cash disbursement slip in the amount of the shortage, or complete a dummy sales slip for the amount of the overage. Then, run the totals again, before making your deposit, and check your permanent change amount.

Although it is not good accounting, if you are only a few cents off, alternatively, you can make up the difference from your pocket, or take it out of the drawer to balance. While this is considered very sloppy bookkeeping, your time is worth more than using it to chase down 10 or 15 cents. You will seldom have significant variances, and these will usually be the result of silly mistakes, like giving both copies of the sales slip to the customer. It is important to balance daily, so that you can pinpoint the date of any variances. This is especially important when you have employees, and when employees and owners work irregular, alternating schedules. Otherwise, there will be questions and suspicions about when the variance occurred and who is responsible.

As you can see, the cash drawer and reconciliation is simple enough that you probably don't even need a cash register unless you are doing an extremely high volume of business. Consider not buying a cash register until you are convinced that the cost will be justified by improvements to your cash reconciliation and controls.

The only real advantage to a cash register is the security of a locking cash drawer. If you want to keep up with inventory on a daily basis, you will still have to use sales slips, since only the most sophisticated point-of-sale computerized cash registers can handle a diverse inventory. A newborn business should not use scarce cash to purchase such a device. Later, when you are on the New York Stock Exchange, or as the technology becomes less expensive, you can add the best computer cash controls with all the bells and whistles your heart desires.

However, if you just can't think of having a business without the presence of a cash register, several models are available for less than $300 that will satisfy basic requirements. Once you have a cash register, you can also use the register tape to verify your manual totals, or vice versa.

Paying Your Bills

Your bank account will look so good, and then it is time to pay the bills. Sometimes, it is even to your advantage to pay a bill ahead of time — the usual time is before 30 days for most vendors — when the manufacturer offers a discount for early payment.

An early-pay discount is usually specified in a notation on your invoice, such as "two percent in ten days." This means you may deduct two percent of the invoice if you pay within ten days. You have to decide whether the savings is worth paying in advance, or if you would be better off to hold payment the full 30 days, thus being able to use the money for a more pressing need.

Most of the time, your invoices from a single manufacturer will not be large enough to realize that great a savings, and only a few manufacturers offer the early payment discount.

Some manufacturers require payment within 10 or 15 days, but these are pretty few and far between. So few, in fact, that you may overlook this fact on their invoices and be late making payment, assuming it is the usual 30-day limit.

Deciding when the 30 days start has always been a bit of a mystery, but to be on the safe side, you should figure this from the date of shipment. If there is a big discrepancy between the date of shipment and the date of arrival, you may want to assume that the clock starts at arrival, and if there is a complaint, you can always explain the situation. Some suppliers try to accelerate payment by backdating their invoices.

By having a net-30 basis on most of your shipments, you have time to sell some of the merchandise before you have to pay for it. This gives you a float time and hopefully enables you to keep your cash flow moving smoothly. There are times when this can get pretty sticky, for instance, when you have been to market and everything you have ordered comes in at once.

Always try to space out shipments at the time you order, but "the best laid plans of mice and men often go awry." Some orders will come before you expect them and others will come much later. Mass arrivals seem to happen when business is the slowest and you have the least amount of cash available, making net-30 accounts even more important.

We decided early on that keeping a good credit record was very important to us and we have not wavered in this thinking. There have been very few occasions when we have not paid a bill on time and usually that was the result of an error on our part. By error, we mean filing the invoice away instead of putting it in our accounts payable file.

When you first open, you can use a very simple method of keeping track of your accounts payable. When an invoice or statement comes in, write it down on a ledger sheet, indicating the manufacturer's name, amount of invoice, date payment is due, and date payment should be mailed, allowing anywhere from three to seven days mail time. Later, indicate on this sheet the date when you pay the bill and the check number. If you check this book each day to see which invoices need to be paid, you will usually avoid missing any payments.

Another method might be to set up an accounts payable filing system, making a folder for each day of the month and putting the invoice in the folder for the day of the month that you need to write the check.

As your sales volume grows, you can switch to a computer for keeping track of your finances, using a program such as the popular *Quicken* software. With a computer, when you receive an invoice, you enter it as a check in the program, postdating the check. Then, you can print checks weekly, setting the program to print all checks due within the following week. Be sure to include the invoice number on each check. This will help if a vendor questions your payment.

A number of computer programs are available for small business accounting, in addition to *Quicken*, that include an accounts payable function. You may want to consider one of these if you have a personal computer and are computer literate. If not, start out with a manual system and convert to computer accounting later if you believe it will be cost-effective.

Keeping on top of your bills is important, so take the time to set up whatever method will be most effective for you. If for some reason you are late in making a payment, it is best to write or call and give a reason for being late. Most manufacturers appreciate the fact that you are conscientious enough to make this effort and will work with you.

A word of caution: Be sure to check each invoice against the shipment because manufacturers do make mistakes. Most manufacturers require that you notify them about any discrepancies within a certain period of time. This includes shortages or breakage in the shipment, as well as bookkeeping errors.

Paying the Government

In addition to taking care of your bills, you also have responsibilities for making your payments to the government. You will be collecting sales taxes and withholding income, Social Security, and Medicare taxes from employees, if you have any, and since these are only paid out monthly or quarterly, it is easy to think you have a healthy bank balance, when, in reality, it is not your money, but Uncle Sam's and the state's.

You will have myriad taxes to pay, so you need to have a reminder system to be sure they are paid when due. These taxes will include income, Social Security, Medicare, withholding, self-employment, unemployment, and sales taxes. You will need to keep track of which taxes must be paid to federal, state, and even local governments. Spend the time necessary to set up a system for ensuring they get paid on time. You should consider setting up a bank account to escrow these funds if you are likely to draw your bank balance down to the point where you are unable to pay your taxes when due.

In our case, we have not set up an escrow, opting to exercise — or at least attempt to exercise — discipline in maintaining sufficient balances to accommodate the tax payments when they become due. It has not been a major problem, but there have been a few unpleasant surprises! You may wish to discuss with your accountant or legal adviser the pros and cons of putting your taxes in an escrow account.

Preventing Cash Crunches

During your first few months in business — and really forever — you should do cash flow projections, as outlined in Chapter 4, and update them monthly. These projections should show both weekly sales projections, as well as weekly anticipated expenses, including payments for rent, merchandise, and taxes, preferably plotted on a graph to show net cash flow, both negative and positive. This will allow you to manage your bank balance to ensure that, at no time, will you be unable to pay your bills.

In actuality, you will probably face times when you will need to put more cash into your business to maintain a positive cash balance. This condition occurs most often before a major seasonal selling period, when you must build your inventory in advance of the anticipated increased sales. In the retail business, the most vulnerable time is in September and October, when you must begin paying for merchandise that has been ordered for the Christmas selling season. By mid-November, sales are usually up enough to replenish the coffers, but it can be touch and go then for a few weeks.

Other cash crunches can occur at income tax time or after you invest in new fixtures, equipment, or an expensive line of goods. It pays to anticipate and plan for these lean times by retaining adequate cash in the business when times are good. Learn to recognize when the large bank balance is really an illusion and needs to be left alone.

Taking Draws

Now that everyone else has been paid and you have planned for maintaining a positive cash balance, you are probably wondering when you will get paid. When you take money out of your business, it is known as a draw.

Don't yield to the temptation to take money out right away, just because you have a large bank balance, without first doing a cash flow analysis. Otherwise, you may find you will just have to put it back in again, when the large monthly bills become due.

Once you establish an average level of profitability for your business over a period of a year or so, you can then begin taking money out at a specific rate, on a regular basis, in line with your average profits. Don't overlook the fact that, for the first year or two, you will probably need to plow a major part of your profits back into the business to build your inventory to more optimal levels, as well as add necessary equipment and fixtures.

Try to resist the temptation to take nickel-and-dime draws on a frequent or irregular basis. These draws are hard to keep track of, and you will find, at year's end, that you have taken out more than you realized and cannot remember where it went.

Reducing Self-Employment Taxes

There are a couple of options for taking money out of the business, while minimizing the impact on your profits. One is through payments to a spouse or other family members for work done in support of the business. If, for example, one spouse is employed outside the business and is paying maximum or near maximum Social Security taxes through the outside employer, you can realize substantial savings in taxes by paying the employed spouse for services rendered to the business, instead of taking it out as profit.

The person who runs the business must pay self-employment taxes on the profits of the business. However, payments to a spouse are deducted from profits, thus you reduce the self-employment tax for the person running the business. The spouse receiving the payments must pay Social Security taxes on them, but not if he or she is already paying the maximum.

Beware that you cannot arbitrarily make payments to your spouse just to avoid taxes. There must be services rendered to the business that are reasonably related to the payments received. See your accountant and the IRS small business tax publications for details.

You are also allowed to pay your children for working at the shop, without deducting taxes, up to a certain amount. Again, check current IRS regulations. This can save you money by transforming allowance money, which you would have to pay anyway, into a deductible business expense. Once again, it must be for work actually performed, or you will be in trouble with Uncle Sam.

Another option is to set up a Simplified Employee Retirement Plan, through which you can pay a percentage of profits into a tax deferred IRA. This is fairly easy to do, but payments must be made to all employees at the same percentage that the owner takes. If you have no employees or a small payroll, this can save you some taxes while you are putting away a retirement fund at the same time.

Check with your accountant about how to set up a retirement fund. For more information about this and other tax-saving tips, refer to the book, *Top Tax Saving Ideas for Today's Small Business*, which is listed in Appendix B.

Success Strategies

That is pretty much it for this painful little exercise of cash management, bill paying, and other payment obligations. It is not all that complicated, but it is one of the most important facets of your business since your discipline — or lack of it — will have a big impact on your profitability, credit rating, and having fewer problems with the government. So get organized, plan carefully, and be diligent in writing those checks on time.

Hopefully, the specific, rather routine, procedures outlined in this chapter will help you manage your daily receipts and disbursements in an orderly, efficient manner, and implement a few tips to hang on to more of your cash receipts.

Daily Reconciliation Worksheet – Instructions

Make enough photocopies of this form to last a year.

Column 1. One line is used for each day that you are open.

Column 2. Total all of your sales slips.

Column 3. Enter the amount of cash left over after you have reestablished the permanent change drawer amount and set it aside.

Column 4. Add up all the cash disbursements or "paid outs" you have made from the cash drawer. These will usually be small, miscellaneous items like janitorial supplies, office supplies, or refunds to customers.

Column 5. Add column 3 and column 4 for your adjusted cash total.

Column 6. Add all of your checks received.

Column 7. Add all your credit card slips for the day.

Column 8. Add columns 5, 6, and 7, then, subtract column 2. The total should be zero. A negative amount indicates a cash shortage, a positive amount indicates an overage. If the shortage or overage is significant, count the cash and run all of the totals again.

Column 9. Add columns 3, 6, and 7. This amount should equal the amount filled out on your bank deposit slip. If credit card receipts are deposited electronically via a terminal, only columns and 3 and 6 will be deposited to your bank account.

Daily Reconciliation Worksheet

1	2	3	4	5	6	7	8	9
Date	Sales Slips Total	Cash Total	Cash Disbursements Total	Adjusted Cash [cols. 3+4]	Checks Total	Credit Card Slips Total	Balance [cols. 5+6+ 7 – col. 2]	Deposit Total [cols. 3+6+7]

Daily Reconciliation Worksheet

1 Date	2 Sales Slips Total	3 Cash Total	4 Cash Disbursements Total	5 Adjusted Cash [cols. 3+4]	6 Checks Total	7 Credit Card Slips Total	8 Balance [cols. 5+6+ 7– col. 2]	9 Deposit Total [cols. 3+6+7]

Chapter 9

Accounting and Computers

Understanding Your Books

When you first set up your books, the first decision you will face is whether to use single- or double-entry bookkeeping. The single-entry system is a simplified accounting system, in which each expense or income item is entered only once. The single-entry method is only slightly more complex than your checkbook. The system involves keeping three basic records.

* Daily cash receipts
* Monthly cash receipts
* Monthly cash disbursements

The double-entry system is slightly more complicated, requiring each item to be entered once as a credit and again as a debit. The advantages of this system are uniformity and having a system of checks and balances, which detects errors and minimizes fraud.

You are not required to use a particular bookkeeping system by the IRS or anyone else unless your business is very large. This may come as something of a surprise to you, since you have probably assumed that Uncle Sam would surely require you to use a system involving complicated paperwork. Given the choice, you can either opt for simplicity, with the single-entry system or the checks and balances that flow from the double-entry method. In a small, owner-managed business, you can probably get by without the benefits — and the extra cost and hassle of the double-entry system. Instead of going into further detail in this book about accounting methods, you can pick up one of the following references:

→ *Small-Time Operator* by Bernard Kamoroff, CPA, for information about single-entry accounting; and

→ *Business Owner's Guide to Accounting and Bookkeeping* by Jose Placencia, Bruce Welge, and Don Oliver for information about double-entry accounting.

Both books contain samples of all the ledgers and worksheets you need to set up your books, along with clear, easy-to-understand instructions on almost everything you will need to know from a financial standpoint. Accordingly, the rest of this chapter will assume that you have one of these references or an equivalent, although other options and methods will be outlined that you may wish to consider, depending on your unique needs and capabilities. You should engage an accountant to review your accounts before you start, especially if you opt for a double-entry system.

We admit we did not hire an accountant at first and had no problems. Maybe ignorance is bliss! We have subsequently had our accountant review our books and he found no problems, although he did suggest some money saving ideas we had not thought of previously.

Two Essential Financial Reports

There are at least two reports that are important to your business, and with which you should be familiar. These are the balance sheet and the profit and loss (P&L) statement. The balance sheet gives you a picture of the net worth of your business, while the P&L statement shows your sales, expenses, and profit for a given period. Examples of both these reports are in the books referenced above, but they do deserve some discussion here.

Balance sheet. The balance sheet is prepared at the end of the year and shows current assets, other assets, current and long-term liabilities, and your net equity in your business. This is very helpful in dealing with your bank on loans and in establishing one measure of your business'

worth if you decide to sell it. The best time to prepare a balance sheet or have your accountant prepare one is at the time you file your income taxes for the year. A typical balance sheet is shown below.

Balance Sheet
XYZ Company
for Period Ending December 31, 1995

Assets

Current assets cash (change drawer)	$ 125.00
Cash in bank	3,878.55
Accounts receivable	0.00
Prepaid rent	1,900.00
Inventory at cost	16,680.76
Subtotal current assets	$22,584.31

Other Assets

Equipment at cost	$ 2,788.49
Less accumulated depreciation	<2,062.07>
Subtotal other assets	$ 726.42
Total assets	$23,310.73

Liabilities

Current liabilities	
Accounts payable	$ 0.00
Current loans	0.00
Long-term liabilities and loans	0.00
Total liabilities	$ 0.00
Net equity in business	$23,310.73

The example shown is a simplified statement, but it generally reflects the condition of a small business that does not owe any money, that pays its bills on time, and that does not extend direct credit. All of these are recommended conditions for a beginning enterprise.

Profit and loss statement. The P&L statement provides useful information on your sales volume, your expenses, and your bottom line — your net profit. It should also be prepared at least annually, but it is a good idea for you to prepare them more often, monthly at first, and at least quarterly thereafter.

These interim reports will likely be only estimates since it is not easy to exactly establish your "cost of goods sold" entry without a physical inventory, and it is usually not practical to do this on a monthly basis unless you have a very small number of items in inventory. You can, however, estimate this cost by reviewing your inventory records or by multiplying your sales by your historical cost-of-goods percentage, which is calculated by subtracting your markup percentage from 100 percent. Inventory management is discussed in Chapter 10.

If you use the keystone markup, your cost of goods will probably vary between 50 and 60 percent of sales. Your expenses will be known, and you can use these figures to calculate your gross profit (gross sales less cost of goods), your total expenses, and your net profit (gross profit less expenses) for each month or quarter. This will be educational — and a little frightening — since your profits will vary significantly, monthly and quarterly. You will probably show losses in some traditionally slow months, such as January. Don't despair, Christmas is coming!

The P&L statement will also enable you to keep an eye on your expenses and take steps to control costs that are getting too high and unduly affecting profitability. Set up your statements to show considerable detail of expenses and compare them to last year's numbers. If you use a computer, your software program, such as *Quicken*, will generate this report for you and even compare the results with previous periods. A sample P&L statement is shown on the next page.

Using the P&L Statement

Using this comparative statement, you can see that although sales were up, so were expenses, causing net profits to increase only a small amount. By scanning the expenses, you can quickly spot those items that increased substantially and perhaps take steps to reduce them.

Your major goal should be to hold the line on expenses, while continuing to increase your sales. Since your gross profit margin will be relatively constant, any increase in sales without a corresponding increase in expenses will result in increased profits.

Profit & Loss Statement

XYZ Company
for Period Ending December 31, 1995

	1994	1995
Gross sales	$95,000.00	$115,000.00
Cost of goods sold	<55,000.00>	<65,000.00>
Gross profit	$40,000.00	$ 50,000.00
Expenses		
Advertising	$ 2,000.00	$ 3,500.00
Car and truck expenses	500.00	800.00
Depreciation	600.00	400.00
Insurance	500.00	500.00
Legal and professional expenses	200.00	200.00
Rent	12,000.00	14,000.00
Office supplies	2,000.00	2,500.00
Taxes	5,000.00	7,000.00
Travel	1,500.00	1,000.00
Meals and entertainment	500.00	300.00
Wages	3,000.00	4,500.00
Miscellaneous	1,500.00	2,500.00
Utilities	1,500.00	1,500.00
Total expenses	$30,800.00	$ 38,700.00
Net profit	$ 9,200.00	$ 11,300.00
Profit (percent of gross sales)	9.7%	9.8%

Most of your expenses, such as rent, utilities, and insurance, will be fixed since you will have to pay these, regardless of your sales. Other expenses, such as wages, supplies, and other miscellaneous expenses, will vary with sales, but not in direct proportion. In other words, a doubling of sales will not cause a doubling of these expenses, although they will increase somewhat. This relationship makes sales volume your key tool to increased profits, provided you have adequate pricing policies and good expense controls.

One of the expenses that is almost totally discretionary also has a major impact on sales volume and is a key indicator to check on a profit and loss statement. That expense is advertising. Your goal should not be to minimize this expense, but rather to raise it to a level that optimizes your sales volume. This, like much of the other advice in this book, is easier said than done. You will have to experiment with the different advertising media and try to find the ones that bring the most sales. As mentioned in Chapter 5, you should strongly consider using an advertising agency to help you find your most productive advertising methods.

Some advertising methods you can try are newspaper, television, radio, hand-distributed flyers, mail-out advertising supplements shared with neighboring businesses, and advertisements sent to your own mailing list. A mailing, though not cheap, always results in measurable increases in sales.

The next most effective advertising for a gift shop is usually radio, followed by TV, with the remaining methods producing so-so results. However, different products and markets demand different advertising methods, so what doesn't work for a gift shop might be just the ticket for you. Try several different methods until you find one that works for you.

By far, our most effective advertising has been our newsletter, which we mail periodically to our own customer mailing list. Shortly after opening, we placed a sign-up sheet in our store, and by now, we have more than 7,000 names of customers interested in our merchandise. We prepare our own newsletters, giving information on sales, new merchandise, and ideas for gifts, and use clip art to create some eye appeal.

One factor that was missing in our initial advertising program was consistency, and we feel sure this cost us in missed sales. We have now developed an advertising program that budgets year-round expenditures.

116

Right from the beginning you will be wise to set up an advertising program and budget for a year in advance. Then, make sure you spend the budgeted monthly amount according to your plan. A ballpark figure you might start with for your initial budget is three to six percent of your estimated or actual gross sales. Then, keep experimenting until you reach optimum levels of sales.

Computerizing Your Books

If you have a personal computer, you should examine the many accounting packages available for small businesses. However, unless you are well-versed in the use of computers and this type of software, setting up and using even a package system may require more time and effort that you can afford to devote to it, given the other demands on your time from a fledgling business. You can always start out manually and switch to a computer after several years in business.

Starting out manually, with a simple system, can be a valuable experience for you and permit you to better understand your business before you attempt to automate it. If you have bookkeeping experience, or are intimately familiar with computers and their software, by all means, go for it! While automation and efficiency are great, simple may be better, at least in the beginning. However, as your business grows, you will probably find that some sort of computer system is essential to maintaining accurate records within the available time.

We have been using our computer increasingly for our records and finances. After reviewing the available software, we purchased Intuit's Quicken, *which is basically a checkbook program. Although it is a simple, single-entry system, we have found it to be very powerful and more than adequate for our accounting needs. We have purchased several of the upgrades to the program as new features are added that we felt we could use. Most of the more complicated accounting packages, including the* QuickBooks *package by Intuit, in our opinion simply have more features — and complications — than a small retail shop owner needs. Most of the more sophisticated reports and analyses available in these packages are simply overkill for a small business such as ours.*

Computers and Software

Today, it is virtually impossible to operate a business of any size without eventually becoming involved with that ultimate modern invention, the computer. Quantum advances have been made in hardware and software and the numbers and affordability of computers and software have increased dramatically, and will likely continue to do so. Even though it is possible to start your business without a computer, the low prices and variety of software titles today almost compels you to computerize at the start if you are computer literate. If you aren't, you should learn. It is not as scary as most folks believe. Using computers can greatly increase your efficiency and allow you to effectively manage a much larger business than otherwise possible. With the rapid advances in technology, you will be faced with two quandaries.

→ Should you buy current models or wait for the next generation?
→ How often should you upgrade?

As usual, there is not really one answer that fits all situations, but here is one strategy that is sound for a small, start-up retail business. First, purchase hardware that is one generation behind, and then skip one or two generations before purchasing an upgrade. The big advantage in doing this is cost, as the older models tend to drop in price as soon as a new microchip is introduced. Not being on the cutting edge of technology is a small price to pay for some significant savings.

Our first computer had an 8086 processor and a 20 megabyte hard drive. It was slow as cold molasses compared to today's models, but at the time it seemed like lightning. About three years later we moved up to a 386SX model with a 107 megabyte hard drive. We now have a 486 model with 66 megahertz processing speed and a 345 megabyte hard drive. It was rendered obsolete with the advent of the Pentium chip. We purchased the 8086 machine just when the 286 models came out, the 386SX when the 486 models came out, and the 486 when Pentiums were introduced. I occasionally lament that my computer is too slow in calculating our monthly inventory, sometimes taking more than two minutes. To which Susie is likely to respond with: "What would you do with an extra two minutes, anyway?" This usually brings me back to reality.

So computerize, but don't try to keep up with the latest technology. Pick a machine that will do the job and stick with it for awhile, upgrading only when significant new features are available at a reasonable price.

What about software? Again, it depends mainly on your knowledge of standard software varieties, such as spreadsheets and databases. If you cannot use the features of these two types of software, then it is better to choose a software package that has been specifically designed for retail stores, or have someone custom design a program for you. Both options are open to you, with the only drawbacks being cost and flexibility. Several package programs for retail are either very expensive or lacking in the flexibility to accommodate your particular operation, or both. But numerous packages are on the market, and it would be a good idea to explore them before you commit to a custom design. For example, some complete systems have been designed for auto, video, hardware, liquor, and other stores, which might fit your needs. You will usually find several software vendors at the merchandise shows at major market centers. Talk to several and ask for demo disks to evaluate their products before buying.

If you do have some database and spreadsheet skills, then you can very easily create systems to control your inventory, payroll, word processing, and general administrative chores. If you have considerable knowledge of these basic programs, you might choose to set up your own systems.

You could use software, such as *Quattro Pro*, *Paradox*, *Wordperfect*, and *Quicken*, as the basic software for managing your business, along with some specialty programs for desktop publishing.

Using *Quattro Pro*, you can set up a spreadsheet for each employee that calculates gross pay, withholding, payroll taxes, and net pay by simply entering hours worked. It also calculates the taxes due to the IRS, and maintains complete records for preparing the quarterly tax reports and the *W-2* forms at year-end. Checks can be written in the *Quicken* program. You can set up tables in *Paradox*, in which you could enter new merchandise received, items sold at each store, and items ordered. From this basic information you can create scripts — simple programs — which produce the following recurring reports:

• Monthly inventory list
• Weekly list of outstanding orders

- Consignor payments due
- Year-end inventory list

In addition, a number of useful reports can be produced when needed, such as a best-sellers list, which gives the dollar sales from all items in descending order over any defined period, an inventory value at any time, value of outstanding orders, and virtually any other information you need to know. You can also use *Paradox* to keep your mailing list and print the labels for your newsletters. As mentioned earlier, the *Quicken* financial program is excellent for money management.

If all this talk about computers is freaking you out, don't despair. You don't have to start out with a computer if it frightens you and you don't have the skills. You can manage effectively without computers, at least until your business has grown to the point that you can master them or until you can afford to hire someone to do it for you. Remember that computers are merely tools for managing more efficiently; they are not ends in themselves. If you can see that they can help you, use them. If not, do it the old-fashioned way until you are convinced they can.

Success Strategies

The very best advice is to keep up with your finances on a monthly basis during your first year of operation, no matter which accounting system you use or how you do it. Make sure you use the profit and loss report to analyze your operation and to make management decisions to improve your financial position. If you lose track of your finances, you will lose valuable time, during which you could have made corrections. In a small, minimally capitalized business, such a loss of reaction time can be disastrous.

While the accounting chores may sound formidable, they are manageable and will become routine if you set up your books carefully and exercise discipline to keep them up on a daily basis. Never fear — you are well able to conquer the accounting monster.

Chapter 10

Inventory
Management

Establishing an Inventory System

One of the most time-consuming and worrisome tasks you will face in operating a retail store is keeping up with your stock. You will almost certainly have several hundred, and possibly several thousand different items in stock. The appropriate business term for all this stuff is inventory. It can also be a verb — and a dirty one, at that — when it is time to count everything.

You will probably have a large number of items in your inventory unless you have a very narrow product mix. You may be able to combine several items from the same vendor under one code if they are the same price and are similar items. For example, you may have stuffed toy bears, cows, and lambs from a single supplier, each priced at $4.50. You can use one code, ABC-1, Stuffed Animal, for all three items. While this simplifies inventory, it limits your ability to correctly appraise the selling potential of the individual items, since they are lumped under one code.

Even after these combinations, you will still likely have 1,500 or more individually coded items with which to deal. This will cause you to spend a significant chunk of time daily on inventory tracking. Which brings up a good question — is it worth it? You will discover, by talking to other retailers, that not everybody keeps up with their inventory on an ongoing basis. Many simply count everything once a year to establish a cost of goods sold and don't bother with it again until the next tax year ends. Some retailers never count their stock, relying instead on estimates to establish the cost of goods.

Since no one is enamored with work for work's sake, you may even consider the idea of abandoning having an inventory system and only counting once a year. After all, if so many people don't do it, why should you? But one of the hard lessons of entering business is that, just because many are doing or not doing a certain thing, does not automatically make it the correct thing to do or not do. You will find that in retailing, as in life, there are some lazy and ineffective operators that do not bear emulating.

When you are the new kid on the block, it is normal to assume that the oldtimers always know the best ways to do things, and your tendency will be to copy them. While it is good to have a certain humility, and be willing to learn from others, it is a mistake to go against good solid principles and your better judgment, even if "everybody does it."

After talking to other retailers and getting to know them, you will discover that there are many bad managers out there along with the good ones. So, don't automatically assume that your ideas are worse than the next person's. Give yourself credit and follow your good judgment. That is why new businesses sometimes succeed while other, older ones are failing.

Inventory Management Advantages

Keeping a current inventory is worth the effort. You will want to establish and maintain a system for tracking your inventory on a daily basis, unless you are selling only nails, screws, jelly beans, or other items with large numbers and low per-item prices.

Some of the advantages of a good inventory tracking system are:

→ Theft control. Without an inventory system, it is impossible to know if you are being ripped off by customers or employees until it is too late. While an atmosphere of trust is the ideal, with no problems with employees and very little shoplifting, it is foolish not to have some safeguards.

→ Customer service. When you keep up with your stock, you can avoid running out of stock constantly, and you can determine if an item is in stock and more readily locate it. You will be surprised at the number of customers that will ask for an item after it is out of stock, and want you to order it for them. Without a good inventory system, you will have a hard time locating an out-of-stock item, price, and manufacturer.

→ Financial management. Inventory systems help you keep track of how you are doing. Would you fly with an airline that sets a course in New York and doesn't check it again until Los Angeles? It makes just as little sense to go for an entire year without knowing the status of your stock.

→ Product tracking. An inventory system allows you to keep track of specific items and weed out low sellers. You can spot slow sellers that are taking up space and move them out with sales or markdowns.

Setting Up a Simple System

To begin with, you can start out with a single card system. Later, you can switch to a computerized system, using software such as the *Paradox* database program for tracking your inventory. However, if you do not have the computer and requisite skills, a card system can be effective, especially as a starter system.

You can purchase 8 x 5 inch, preprinted inventory cards from your office supply store or you can photocopy the blank Stock Record card at the end of this chapter onto index paper and use it. These cards have spaces for the item code, description, supplier, cost, selling price, beginning stock, sales, and current balance. They are printed on both sides, and each card will normally last for up to a year or more of normal sales.

When a new item arrives, assign a unique inventory code, enter a description, your cost, selling price, and the amount of your beginning stock. A really simple coding system is to use alpha-numeric codes, with the first one to four digits being an abbreviation of the vendor's name, followed by an item number. For example, items from a company called Homespun Cottage could be coded HC-1, HC-2, and so on.

You have to be careful not to duplicate previous codes because many manufacturers have similar names within an industry. Once you have the card filled out, then, file the card alphabetically by its inventory code in a card tray.

A typical Stock Record card is laid out as follows:

Stock Record – Sample

Inventory Number: _AS-19_   Vendor: _ABC Sales_

Description: _Teddy Bear_   Minimum Stock Level: _6_

Manufacturer's Stock Number: _665_   Maximum Stock Level: _12_

Cost: _$9.75_   Retail Price: _$19.75_

Ordered			Received and Sold			
Date	P.O. #	Quantity	Date	Received	Sold	Balance
1-3-96	1234	8	1-10-96	8		8
			1-11-96		3	5
1-12-96	5678	5	1-19-96	5		10
			1-20-96		5	5

Your next step is to set up vendor files for each vendor, where you can file catalogs, brochures, and invoices. This way, you can go straight to the vendor's file from your inventory cards.

When an item is sold, the inventory code is listed on the sales ticket. During the day or at the end of the day, the inventory cards are updated from the sales tickets. Obviously, this requires pricing each item individually, with a tag or sticker showing the code. This can be a sizeable task when you receive a large order, but it is worth it. With some small, low-cost items, this is impractical, so, in that case, you can post the code on the bin or container. These items are usually located near the checkout counter, for convenience and for security purposes.

Even if you use a computer, you can still use the same sales tickets, merchandise coding, daily posting, and pricing systems. The only difference is that you will enter the daily sales and receipts on a computer-generated printout, which is then input into the computer on a monthly basis. Each month, you update the inventory and generate a new printout for the succeeding month.

A handy item to purchase is a pricing gun, which is capable of mechanically printing your price codes on the price stickers. This can provide much improved efficiency in pricing merchandise, especially for multiple items. A pricing gun will also eliminate many errors resulting from misreading several different handwriting styles. If you use an alpha-numeric inventory coding system, you will find that standard pricing guns may not accommodate your system. However, most companies will make a custom imprint wheel to accommodate your system for a reasonable charge.

Managing Your Inventory System

Now that you understand the mechanics of the inventory system, you will need to determine some policies and procedures for actually managing your inventory, using the system. Obtaining knowledge about your inventory is useless unless you use this information to improve your store's sales and profitability. Review your inventory on a daily basis as you post sales, and watch for these indicators.

→ Items that are selling well and have low stock balances. With this type of item, you will find it helpful to establish and indicate on the inventory card — or computer sheet — a desirable reorder point, allowing time for shipping. For example, if you sell an average of two of a certain item per month, and it takes a month to reorder and receive a new shipment, then the reorder point would be when you are down to two items in stock — or three, if you want to keep a margin of safety.

→ Slow sellers that have been in inventory a long time. Unless these are seasonal items, which will sell later, you should consider putting them on sale. Mark them down to move them out so you can put your money into other, faster-moving items. Be brutal here, marking them down until they move, even if you have to take a loss. This is painful, but it must be done!

→ Hot sellers for which sales have increased. For these items, you should increase your order quantities, or put in a special order, to take advantage of the selling surge. You have to strike while the iron is hot!

In addition to your daily checks, you should also thoroughly review all your inventory items, at least quarterly, to look for the same indicators mentioned above. Note the poor sellers and use these items as the main attractions in periodic sales.

You do not want to run a continuous sale unless you are in the discount business, but you can plan maybe three sales each year to get rid of slow-moving merchandise and to boost sales during slow times of the year. Another option is to periodically maintain a sale table, on which items are placed for quick sale.

Some examples of sales themes you can use for your regular periodic sales are:

- After Christmas sale, during which you sell all unsold Christmas items at half-price, usually lasting only a week or two;
- Valentine's Day sale the week before Valentine's Day, during which you give ten percent off anything heart-shaped or with a heart on it — and also mark down your slow movers; and
- Gambler's sale, which is a good inventory clearance sale for late summer. During the sale week, mark down your ugly ducklings 10 percent per day, starting on Monday, so that by Saturday, they are 60 percent off.

The gambler's sale stimulates a lot of interest as customers gamble on when to buy a coveted item, at the lowest price, without losing it to someone else. Always send out a flyer to your mailing list to publicize this sales event, so your regular customers can come in to spot items they want. This sale can be a good way to clear out stock before the Christmas season.

When you have a sale, do not group your sale merchandise in one location in the store, except for a sale table of seasonal merchandise. Instead, place brightly colored stickers on the sale items throughout the store. This exposes the sale shopper to your regular priced merchandise and encourages the purchase of more than just marked-down items.

Physical Inventory

The final inventory activity you will need to deal with is the annual physical inventory. Despite some merchants' practices to the contrary, the physical inventory is essential to the prudent financial management of your store and should not be skipped. You must do this at the end of your tax year, which is almost always the calendar year. You might close one or two days at year end, even working on New Year's Day if you don't care that much for football.

There is not much to say here, except that it is a lot of work. To get started, you can make lists from your inventory system before the physical count and use these to make your count. These lists should include the item code, the cost per item, and the inventory quantity shown on the records, along with a space beside each item for the actual count and a space for the total value of that item in stock, as shown below.

Inventory List – Sample

Item	Code	Cost per Item	Inventory Quantity	Actual Quantity	Value
Wooden sign	AA-01	$ 3.50	5	4	$ 14.00
Teddy Bear	AS-19	9.75	8	7	68.25
Fruit Basket	AT-13	12.50	2	2	25.00
T Kitchen	AT-14	10.00	10	10	100.00
Wreath, Pansy	AT-15	8.50	1	1	8.50
Pillow	BA-09	2.50	2	2	5.00
Angel	CL-03	3.50	2	2	5.00

After the count, you calculate the value by multiplying the cost times the actual count. This column is then totalled for all items to give the total inventory value. With a manual system, you do this by hand, but a computerized inventory system can calculate the values, along with differences between actual and recorded inventory. By comparing the actual versus calculated inventory, you will have an idea of the loss of goods through theft or disappearance.

You will likely decide it is easier to start at one end of the store and move through each section systematically, counting everything as you go. Or maybe you can come up with a better way.

Success Strategies

In general, keeping up with your inventory will be a boring, time-consuming activity that you will be tempted to neglect. To do so, however, will be to lose control over a function that is one of the key factors to successful retailing and to a profitable, well-managed business. Do so at your peril. Instead of treating the task as drudgery, try to look at the activity as providing variety to your life. Or, consider inventory tasks as the price you pay for having to go shopping at all these fun and exciting market centers and having to open up packages of interesting goodies that arrive at your store periodically. However you look at it, make sure to do the inventory.

Stock Record

Inventory Number: _____   Vendor: _____

Description: _____   Minimum Stock Level: ____

Manufacturer's Stock Number: ____   Maximum Stock Level: ____

Cost: _____   Retail Price: _____

| Ordered | | | | Received and Sold | | | |
Date	P.O. #	Quantity		Date	Received	Sold	Balance

Chapter 11

Employment Relationships

Choosing Your Workforce

Depending on the kind of business you enter, your dealings with others who work with you in your business may consist solely of supervising your own children as part-time employees; solely working with your spouse; or recruiting, training, scheduling, and providing daily supervision of a dozen or more people. Each of these employment relationships have unique problems that occur, as well as having certain principles that apply in all situations. This chapter discusses some of the problems you may encounter with your various types of employment relationships.

> *In addition to working with each other, we have benefited from hiring our teenager and have also employed up to five other employees on a full- and part-time basis. We have, therefore, avoided the major hassles inherent in a large workforce.*

Your Children

Supervising your own children in your business will involve a degree of pain and suffering that you have experienced many times over. Employing your offspring is a common practice that seems to offer many advantages, but as in most family matters, may not be as desirable as it appears. Hark back, now, to those days of yesteryear, when it took you longer to coax and threaten that youngster into mowing the lawn or cleaning the house than it would have taken to do it yourself. But, as parents, you owed it to the child to teach him or her a lesson in self-discipline and industriousness. Well, you will have some of the same problems with your children working in the business.

You might think because they are getting paid now and you are not in a parent-child role, but an employer-employee relationship, that this will make a difference. But, kids are smart. They know that, despite what you say, you are still good old Mom and Dad, and they can still manipulate you as they have done successfully for so many years. So, don't fool yourself that you can eliminate the parental role from the business relationship. Your children will not hesitate to:

• Ask to leave early to go out with friends;
• Request an advance on next week's wages; or
• Tell you how you should operate the business.

These insights should not discourage you from using your children in the business, as it still has many positive aspects. However, you must dispel any illusions you may have about the ability to separate business from family.

Our son proved very good at handling money and dealing with customers. This experience allowed him to secure a steady job as a checker for a supermarket chain, where he was able to continue his experience in an employee and employer relationship that is more realistic and demanding, which is something that is not really possible in the family business. Later on, when he was a junior in college studying radio and TV, he was able to contribute significantly by writing and providing voice-overs for our TV commercials.

The positive aspects of employing your children are:

→ Enjoying the economic benefit of having your children work for the money they receive from you and being able to deduct their wages from your before-tax business income;

→ Providing hands-on, valuable job experience and training for your children; and

→ Spending more time together as a family, albeit in the business setting.

Your Spouse or Partner

Many small retailers are mom-and-pop operations. While this is not a new innovation, the media has recently shown an increased interest in this new genre of spousal business enterprises. If you plan to extend your marital relationship into the business arena, you will need to consider several issues and establish some ground rules. Even if you are partners with someone other than a spouse, or you are in business alone, many of the principles still apply to your relationships with your partner or manager.

The first bit of advice is not to believe that a joint business venture can or will salvage a shaky marriage. This may seem obvious, but when you consider that couples have children in the hope that a baby will draw them closer and solve marital disputes, it is not unreasonable to assume that some people may believe that a business relationship will do likewise.

This concept is roughly equivalent to a ship's captain deciding that the best way to save a ship that has hit an iceberg is to begin an intensive effort to relocate all the deck chairs and inventory the supplies. It might divert attention from the real problem for awhile, but it won't fix it, and sooner or later the boat will sink, albeit with a neat deck and up-to-date inventories.

Therefore, if your marriage has problems, fix them before you engage in activities that will merely divert attention from them. If you cannot function as a team in your personal relationship, it is unlikely you will function any better by adding the additional dimension of a business relationship.

It also seems prudent not to enter into business together at the same time that you get married, unless you know each other very, very well. Your first couple of years as newlyweds will require many adjustments just to resolve those major issues involving in-laws, finances, sex, and whether the toothpaste tube should be squeezed from the bottom or middle. Adding the stress caused by a new business would be unfair to the marriage, as well as the adjustments to marriage being detrimental to the potential for business success.

Another consideration is whether or not both spouses have personality traits that allow them to enjoy or at least tolerate a close relationship 24 hours a day. If one or both of you has a need for a lot of psychological space or is basically a loner who requires solitude and distance for long periods of time, a business joint venture may be doomed to failure, or at least may guarantee misery to one or both of you. Some marriages survive in spite of vastly differing personality traits and psychological needs because separate work interests and activities provide a safety valve. Take away the safety valve by combining work and play, and you can have an explosion.

Even with these caveats, a spousal business partnership can be a rewarding, fulfilling experience that can strengthen and enrich a marriage. If your marriage is in good shape and you follow some guidelines to minimize conflict, a spousal business venture can be a great idea. Notice that conflict can be minimized, not avoided, since conflict is inevitable when two people live and work closely together. Some rules that serve to reduce friction are described below.

First rule. The first rule is to decide in advance who will be responsible for what, based on each spouse's individual capabilities. This implies a degree of knowledge, based on a realistic self-assessment, devoid of both egotism and self-deprecation. In other words, don't assume you know and can do everything better; and conversely, don't play the "I'm more humble than you" game. Becoming a successful businessperson requires a healthy self-image!

After the division of labor is made, each spouse must respect the other's responsibility and authority. That is not to imply that there are to be rigid lines that must never be crossed, since it is also important to communicate and consult on important issues and reach a consensus, where possible. But, in the final analysis, the responsible partner's decision must be respected. Otherwise, you will wind up with a lot of tie votes, and the decision-making process is stalemated.

In our case, for example, I am an engineer, and although I am generally outgoing and get along with people well, I am not blessed with a lot of originality and artistic creativity. I am a logical thinker, have considerable experience in financial and personnel management, and am good at organizing and problem solving. In addition, I have passable carpentry and mechanical skills.

Susie, on the other hand, is quite creative and skilled at most crafts and needlework. She has an innate talent for tasteful decorating, and, like most women, is more closely attuned to feelings and intuition.

Therefore, we divided up the responsibilities such that she is responsible for the displays, the buying of merchandise, and the day-to-day operation of the shop, including customer relations. I set up the books, do the financial accounting, and accompany Susie on buying trips to keep track of expenditures and act as "go-fer" for her — which took some getting used to. Although we occasionally meddle in each other's business — and get our hands slapped — we have been pretty successful in maintaining respect for each other's territory.

Second rule. The second rule is not to try to impose your own particular style or idiosyncrasies on your partner. Don't insist that everything be done in the same way you would do it. Even though you are working together, you should still allow each other some space, and some latitude to work in the way that is most comfortable to your partner.

As mentioned above, I am an organizer, while Susie is more of a free spirit, who tends to concentrate on creative things or customer service at the expense, sometimes, of neatness. Some of our more notable disputes have arisen when I come be-bopping into the store, criticizing the untidy appearance of the checkout desk, or the files, usually at the end of a particularly busy day of dealing with customers.

After being burned a few times by the resulting flareups, I have decided that neatness still counts, but it isn't as critical as continuing to live! On the other hand, Susie has learned to be more methodical in handling and filing the tax forms and payroll records I use to keep up with the financial reporting.

Third rule. The third rule is to maintain some separateness. That may sound contradictory to marital closeness, but every human being needs some time to themselves to pursue their own interests, or simply do nothing. Don't insist that you share every waking moment. You can accomplish this by taking some time away from the shop, separately.

> *I have a part-time "other job" so this is accomplished that way for me, while Susie takes two days off during the week to spend shopping, staying home, or whatever.*

Even if both of you work full-time in the business, arrange to take some time off, separately. Too much togetherness can be stifling!

Fourth rule. The fourth rule is to maintain some other mutual interest besides your business. Couples who are in business together often are so wrapped up in it that they are unable to think or talk about anything else. This becomes very boring to friends and family, resulting in isolation of the couple and a narrow lifestyle that is difficult to sustain. So, do something else, preferably together. Join a bowling league, the local symphony society, a neighborhood association, church, or anything that you both enjoy and are interested in.

> *We are both active in our church and Sunday school, which provides us an opportunity for socializing and for putting our religious faith into action through a variety of activities. Try not to allow the business to intrude into this area of your lives. It is not easy at times since a business can become an all-consuming passion if you are not careful.*

Fifth rule. The fifth rule is to maintain your family relationships as first priority. Tragic results occur when parents allow their business interests to supplant their responsibilities to their children. Children require a considerable amount of time and effort from their parents in order to fulfill their needs for security and guidance, especially during the elementary and adolescent years. If you are not there for them, they will find others who are, and they may not be the best role models.

We chose to wait until our children were in high school to begin our business, and even then, there were times when we were not able to do a good job both as parents and businesspersons.

If you enter business with young children, it is manageable, but it will require commitment and careful planning to be good parents and successful entrepreneurs. Many of you are probably old enough to have children and aging parents, and this combination can bring a great deal of stress into your lives, in addition to the normal stresses of operating a business.

Think carefully about your life situation in relationship to the timing of your entry into business ownership. Don't become discouraged, but make a commitment to take care of family responsibilities first and factor the necessary extra time and effort into your plans.

Sixth rule. The sixth and final rule is to always reserve some time to be together. Remember that marriages require time and attention to maintain good, quality, caring relationships. Don't let your business rob you of your intimacy. You don't necessarily have to exclude business discussions from this shared time. In fact, some of your most meaningful time together may be spent on buying trips, discussing your plans, hopes, and dreams. Speaking of which, it is important to have dreams that are shared with your partner, so you should talk about them and be sure you both are pursuing the same goal.

The partnership in which one spouse is longing for millionaire status through continued expansion, while the other assumes a quiet, modest existence in an owner-operated business is in for trouble when the conflicting dreams are discovered. Spend time together checking out and comparing those dreams, so you can follow them together. While business discussions are okay during your time together, don't neglect time for fun, foolishness, and sex — not necessarily in that order. Remember, businesses can come and go, but a good marriage is a jewel to be cared for and treasured.

Couples should consider acquiring insurance on each other to insure that the business can continue in the absence of one of the partners. This is not a pleasant thought to contemplate, but it is a prudent step to prepare for unforeseen events.

The positives can far outweigh the negatives in husband and wife partnerships. Hopefully, you will find that your business relationship enhances and complements your personal lives if you decide to combine business with matrimony.

Your Employees

You may be tempted to rely totally on yourselves and your family for employees. This is a mistake — sooner or later, you will find that situations, such as illness, vacations, deaths in the family, or just plain fatigue, will require the use of outside help. It is better to have someone trained and ready for such an event. If you can have several people available for part-time, on-call employment, so much the better.

In our case, we chose part-time help from customers who showed interest and potential as employees and trained them over a period of time. We now have a full-time manager along with three part-time employees who can operate the shop as well as we can, on a daily basis. We use the part-time employees two or three days a week during most of the year, more during peak seasons.

Communicate policies and procedures. Communicating your policies and procedures to your employees is important. That way, when you are not present, you can be assured that the business will be operated in accordance with your philosophy. This is why you should have your house rules, as outlined in Chapter 7, written down and given to your employees. While you may be able to get away without doing this if you have few employees and work closely with them on a daily basis, it is definitely a necessity if you have more than two or three employees, or if you have more than a one-shift operation. You should also work with new employees until you are confident of their performance.

Complaints about your employees. You will inevitably have complaints about your employees from some customers. These can be very delicate situations that you must handle carefully. When a customer complains, always remember that there are at least two sides to every story. So, refrain from forming an opinion as to who is right or wrong until you have heard the other side. It is appropriate to assure the customer of your intent to check into the situation and to correct any problems.

If you run a small shop and are normally in the store much of the time, expect that some customers will always want to deal with you, personally, and will resent having to do business with your employees. This can result in unfair accusations against your employees by customers attempting to force you to pay more attention to them and cater to them. In simple terms, some customers have a need to always deal with the boss because it inflates their own egos and, in their minds at least, gives them some special status.

Don't allow them to appeal to your ego by telling you how much better you are than your employees. Resist the temptation to bask in the glow of their praise and say something negative about a valued employee. A good response in such situations is to say something positive about your employee, such as, "We have been very pleased with Joe's work. He has been a real asset to our business." While you will probably have to give special attention to such customers, don't let them dominate you and tell you how to run your business and treat your employees.

When you have a customer complain about an employee, it is also appropriate to apologize for anything that might have offended the customer and to reinforce your desire that everyone feel comfortable and well-treated in your store. It is inappropriate to summon the employee and deal with the situation in front of the customer. That should be done in private, and in a nonthreatening atmosphere. Remember that good employees are more valuable than an unreasonable customer, and be prepared to give your employee the benefit of the doubt. On the other hand, be prepared to take prompt, firm action to correct inappropriate behavior.

The best way to approach the situation with your employee is to wait for the proper time, simply inform your employee of the customer's complaint, and allow for a response. If you believe the employee acted improperly, try to deal with the behavior and do not attack the employee personally. If it is the first time this behavior has occurred, simply suggest a different, acceptable way of dealing with similar situations in the future. If the same behavior persists, you should continue to discuss performance improvements with the employee and document your directions to the employee in writing, being sure to keep a copy.

Dismissals. If improvement is not forthcoming, you should consider dismissing the employee, again documenting your reasons in writing, for the employee and for your records. If the employee files for unemployment compensation or files a suit or discrimination complaint, it is important to have documentation to defend your actions. This documentation should demonstrate that you informed your employee of unacceptable performance, allowed opportunity for improvement, and provided necessary training in job duties. If time and your budget allows, have your attorney review your proposed action before you do it.

Of course, some offenses warrant immediate dismissal, such as theft, violence, and use of drugs and alcohol on duty. You should have strong evidence of these offenses, however, and document your actions thoroughly. This is a litigious society, and more and more employees are suing employers over dismissals and disciplinary actions, so be prepared to defend your actions.

Most states have fairly liberal unemployment compensation laws, but most allow for disqualification of employees who are dismissed for misconduct. Since your business' experience in this regard determines your unemployment tax rate, you should oppose payments to employees dismissed for misconduct. You will be notified when an employee claims benefits, and be given an opportunity to appear if you wish to oppose payments.

You may be tempted to just let it go, but your tax rate will go up, and it will take a long time to get it back to normal. Consult your attorney for specific procedures in your state for opposing a claim.

Employment Laws

Myriad laws and regulations that you should be aware of govern employee work hours, benefits, and treatment. Contact your local labor department office and your state employment agency to obtain specific requirements governing your particular situation. Unless you employ substantial numbers of people, your responsibilities will be relatively simple and easy to administer.

Most states will require you to register as an employer with various departments. Check with your business assistance center or labor department to see about registration. You will also have to follow other labor-employment laws, including those for:

- Family and medical leave;
- Workers' compensation insurance;
- Occupational safety and health;
- Wage-hour requirements, such as minimum wage, child labor, overtime pay, and rest and meal periods;
- Anti-discrimination; and
- Mandatory posters that need to be displayed at your place of business.

Often, the appropriate agencies will find you and get the necessary information to you once you obtain an employer identification number and begin paying taxes to the IRS. But, it is your responsibility to comply with labor laws. The three most important things you absolutely must do to stay in compliance with the law are described below.

→ Calculate and deduct applicable payroll taxes. First, you must deduct Social Security, Medicare, and federal income taxes from all employees, regardless of how little or infrequently they work.

→ Deposit your tax payments and payroll deductions. The second, and more important requirement is that you must deposit the taxes deducted from employees, along with your share, on the schedule prescribed by the IRS, which varies according to the amount collected. Check with them for the schedule applicable to your operation. Numerous small businesses are ultimately shut down by the IRS for failure to pay their payroll taxes. Do not neglect this aspect of employee management.

→ Verify eligibility for employment. The third requirement from Uncle Sam involves completing and maintaining a form that documents the nationality or immigration status, or both, of all employees. The U.S. Immigration and Naturalization Service can provide guidance here.

Your state also will probably require you to withhold state income taxes and pay unemployment insurance on all your employees. Just as with the IRS, you must make sure to pay the state revenue department.

You cannot treat occasional workers as "contract labor" and avoid these taxes. Remember all those cabinet nominees in President Clinton's administration who had to withdraw because of the "Nanny" problem? The only people who qualify as contract labor are those who furnish their own tools and work on something other than an hourly or salaried basis. The bottom line is: Retail store workers don't qualify as contract labor.

Success Strategies

Employee relations can be summed up in a couple of statements.

→ First, always treat employees with respect, give them the benefit of the doubt, ensure that you train them properly, and communicate regularly and clearly with them.

→ Second, provide them the tools they need to do their job; give them a safe, pleasant environment in which to work; and pay them a decent wage.

Don't expect adults with significant skills and experience to run your store in your absence at minimum wage. Check around your area for prevailing wage practices, but don't be overly eager to get by with the minimum. A competent, dependable employee is worth a reasonable wage. You can also give your employees perks, such as discounts of 10 to 20 percent off on your merchandise. You might also consider setting up a simplified employee pension IRA, as mentioned in Chapter 8, and offer group health insurance if it is feasible.

You will experience virtually no problems with your employees if you consider them your friends and equals and treat them as such.

Chapter 12

Wrapping
It Up

Maintain Perspective

If ever there was a business in which it is easy to fall into the trap of "not seeing the forest for the trees," it is retailing. It is a business in which you literally live or die with each day's sales unless you are a very, very disciplined individual. This is doubly true if you are the owner and manager of a retail store. Why is this so?

An article ridiculing the fancy job descriptions bureaucrats create for themselves gave the following description: "The incumbent in this position makes irrevocable decisions involving interstate commerce. Decisions must be made immediately and are not subject to review by higher authority. Wrong decisions can result in millions of dollars in damages." What was this seemingly high-level executive job? The description was for a flagger on a highway construction project.

While this job description obviously exaggerates the importance of the flagger, it can certainly be applied to a retail store manager. That is why it is so hard to keep a global perspective when you are in the midst of an operation in which you must make instant decisions, take sole responsibility for them, and see the results at the end of each and every day in the form of the day's sales. Is it any wonder that you feel like you are on an emotional roller coaster? During your first few months in business, you will likely go home either depressed or elated because of the day's receipts.

Perhaps no other business has as many variables and so much un-predictability that gets translated into such immediate, measurable results. In manufacturing, you have contracts on which you can plan for months or even years. In a service business, you book your work in advance. But in retailing, you open the store each day, without any earthly idea who will come, whether they will buy anything, and if you will cover expenses. While there are seasonal sales cycles, you have absolutely no way of knowing what a particular day or week will bring in the way of sales. You are literally at the mercy of the weather, changing trends, and the individual idiosyncrasies of people.

Are they in a buying mood or not? Will today's good weather motivate them to shop or go to the lake? Is this payday for a lot of people? Is the national economy in a recession or a boom? What did the stock market do today? The answers to these and a hundred other questions hold the key to your sales volume for a given day and can determine your mood unless you take a longer perspective.

Develop a Business Plan

After this seemingly bleak picture, you may wonder if there is any valid reason for attempting to do any business planning. The answer is a resounding "Yes!" Even though there is little predictability on a day-to-day or even week-to-week basis, you can count on predictability in overall consumer demand and the buying habits of consumers in general. This means that, unless you are in a totally atypical selling environment, you will be able to count on and plan for a reasonably stable demand for your products, provided you have done a good job of selecting a product line and location.

The key is not to become mired in the emotions of daily sales figures, but to plan for the long term and carry through with those plans despite the daily see-sawing of receipts. That is called maintaining your perspective.

An old proverb states that if you don't have any particular destination, you should have no trouble getting there. You should, therefore, develop a business plan, set some goals and objectives, and craft a reporting system to tell you if your plan is succeeding. This business plan includes the planning, researching, and forecasting discussed in Part I. But, your plan should also set some goals with respect to the overall results you expect to achieve. You should be able to answer these questions.

→ What level of sales do you expect to reach in the first year?

→ What percent of growth do you want for each succeeding year?

→ How much profit do you want to make the first year and thereafter?

You may say you have no idea how to predict such things, but you must if you are to intelligently plan your business operation. Do some research at your library, talk to other merchants, consult national business periodicals, and set some realistic but challenging goals. Don't think too small since most people seldom rise above their expectations.

Monitor Your Progress

Once you set your goals, implement a system to monitor your progress. Keep up with sales on a monthly and quarterly basis, along with expenses and profit margins. Compare the results with your plan. If you meet your goals, celebrate — go out for dinner. If you don't meet them, don't panic. Remember that you should not place too much stock in short-term performance because it can be skewed by so many of the factors mentioned above. If, on the other hand, you are actually falling behind, try to make adjustments to your operation.

When we started our business, we set a goal of increasing our sales 10 percent a year, and maintaining net profit margins between 10 and 15 percent. We have generally achieved our sales goals, but we are still on the low end of the profit range. As we perceived that we were falling short of our goals, we have taken steps to improve. We moved our location after three years to get in a higher traffic location and save on rent. We have worked on improving our gross profit by trying to include freight costs in our markup, where possible. We have also embarked on an increased emphasis on advertising to try to keep up with our plan for increased sales.

If sales are lower than planned, explore the possibility of increasing your advertising. If your profit margin is lower than planned, take a look at your pricing policies to see if you can improve profit without affecting sales by raising prices just slightly. Look into the possibility of moving your store or of opening other outlets. After all your investigations, you may discover a reason beyond your control, such as worsening local economic conditions.

Check with other merchants to see if they are having the same experience. If so, maybe the only thing to do is hunker down, cut expenses as much as you can, and ride it out. Remember, in selling as in physics, what goes up must come down, and vice versa. You can at least be postured to take advantage of the upturn when it does occur.

The point is, you should have projections and plans for your business. If you achieve them, great! If not, you will be in a better position to make corrections or to roll with the punches you can't control or anticipate. Step back from the trees and take a look at the forest. Remember, you are not in business for a day or a week, but for the long haul, and you need to keep that all-important perspective.

Benefits and Disadvantages

Hopefully, this book has filled in many of the gaps in information available to novice entrepreneurs and provided guidance as you contemplate whether or not retailing is for you. As you plan and actually implement your entry into the most treasured American dream, owning your own business, you will still face many unanswered questions and problems. However, you will also receive many rewards.

Starting and managing a Sears store is a great deal different than struggling, with limited resources, to open a small mom-and-pop retail store. While the principles are the same, it is somewhat intimidating to try to follow Harvard Business School instructions, when you know in your heart that you are not, and probably never will be, a business mogul.

In your venture, you will need to deal with more clear, down-to-earth solutions and specific details of starting a small business, complete with the frustrations, difficulties, and rewards thereunto appertaining, as they say on those MBA diplomas. All of the answers are not in this book, but if you continue the learning process yourself and are always willing and eager to listen to new and different ideas, you will have what it takes to survive.

You will experience many mixed emotions — that is what you feel when your daughter comes home at 3:00 A.M. carrying a Gideon Bible — as you develop your business. Nurturing your business will require considerable time and effort, and you will ask yourself many times if it is worth it. You will talk about selling out, usually right after a particularly trying day at work or in a cash flow crunch.

So far, neither of us has reached the point where we felt we wanted to quit. Why? The answer is complex, and not easily put into words. We have been successful in the sense that we have always shown a profit, but the amount of the profits have not been such as to allow us to retire to Florida. We like the work, generally, but it also gets tiring and sometimes very b-o-r-i-n-g.

The main reason entrepreneurs like you stick with it has to do with a sense of accomplishment and pride of ownership you will get from no other venture. You will be proud of your business that you actually started from scratch — a business you are maintaining and that people really seem to like and are willing to support with their money. You will also like attaining a certain measure of control over your life, unlike what is available from a conventional job that puts you in a position of subservience to an organization whose goals and objectives may or may not coincide with your own.

As people approach that mid-life point, begin to evaluate their accomplishments to date, and compare their ultimate goals with the time remaining to accomplish them, they generally conclude that there is a gap between expectations and reality. Owning your own business provides an alternative means of accomplishment.

In addition, you will enjoy the opportunity to become a part of a community, by meeting and establishing friendships with many people with whom you would otherwise not have come in contact. Other, more direct benefits are opportunities to work closely with others, such as your spouse, traveling to the merchandise markets, and getting to see more of this country.

Although you may not become rich, you may be able to use your profits to help with family finances, supplement college expenses, and most importantly, build an equity that will hopefully be available to provide for some extra security in your retirement years.

Lest you fixate on this euphoric ending and ride off into the sunset, a more honest appraisal is that, for all you will gain from this experience, you will also have to give up some things — things like freedom to take vacations when other normal people do, be home for supper with the family every night, and be available for your kids as much as you would like. With older children, you can probably maintain a reasonably good relationship, but for those with young children, retailing may result in your spending less time with them than they need to cope successfully with the trials of adolescence or childhood.

Success Strategies

Finally, if you have decided retail is for you, here are some dos and don'ts to consider.

→ Do evaluate your reasons for wanting to start a business.

→ Do be realistic about the cost of starting a business, and be sure you are capable of acquiring the necessary funds.

→ Do evaluate the personal cost of investing a good portion of your life in a business.

→ Do try to apply the information contained in this book to your own personal situation, instead of assuming that what worked for one business will work for you.

→ Don't be intimidated by the statistics about business failures if you really want to try.

→ Don't listen to all the free advice you will get from those who have never gotten into the game or have dropped out.

→ Don't give up too easily, after you start.

Now, it is up to you.

❖ Part IV ❖

The Appendices

Appendix A
Glossary of Terms

Appendix B
Useful Publications

Appendix C
Market, Gift, and Design Centers

Appendix D
Exhibition Companies and Trade Associations

Index

Glossary
of Terms

Assets. These are the items of value that your business owns, such as property, equipment, cash, and accounts receivable. They can also include such intangibles as trade names, goodwill, and mailing lists.

Balance sheet. A financial report that lists the assets, liabilities, and net worth of your business.

Cash flow. The movement of cash, checks, and negotiable instruments into and out of your bank account at a given time or period of time. If it is positive, you have enough money to pay bills, and if negative, you don't.

COD. Literally, cash on delivery. Frequently these are the terms of your first order from a new vendor, and for some manufacturers, all orders. Payment includes not only the cost of goods and shipping costs, but an additional fee for processing the transaction. This latter fee is called the COD charge.

Collateral. Something of value you are required to pledge as security for a loan and generally required to obtain credit at a bank, unless the banker is your mother.

Consignment. The process of taking goods for sale in your store, without paying for them until sold. They remain the property of the consignor until sold, at which time an agreed-upon percentage of the total selling price is retained by the store, with the remainder paid to the consignor.

Cost of goods. A technical term for the cost of purchasing or man-ufacturing the items you sell. Includes freight costs but not expenses such as rent, utilities, and office supplies. Consult the IRS' *Publication 334* for a detailed definition.

Double-entry bookkeeping. A system of keeping up with your fi-nances involving the entry of each expense and income as a debit and a credit. The system was most likely designed by accountants to confuse mere mortals, and require that you hire them to keep your books. The system does provide checks and balances to detect errors and minimize fraud and deception.

Draw. A term meaning to take money out of your business as profit or payment to yourself if you are the sole proprietor. It includes the value of merchandise you remove for your own use.

Employer identification number (EIN). An IRS assigned number you must obtain before employing other persons in your business. Used by Uncle Sam to make sure you pay the required payroll taxes and withhold income taxes from your employees' wages.

Entrepreneur. One who endeavors to provide a service or product to others for a profit. Involves risk and, often, innovative approaches.

Escrow. An account set up to collect and disburse funds for a par-ticular purpose. It identifies the funds and maintains a sufficient bal-ance to make payments, when due. Often used to maintain sales and payroll taxes in a separate account to ensure they don't get lost in your overall bank balance.

Expenses. These are the so-called overhead costs of operating your business, as distinguished from cost of goods, as defined above. Includes such items as employee wages, postage, rent, insurance, and all other on-going costs of remaining open for business.

Finish-out. The structural, mechanical, electrical, and decorating cost of transforming new or previously occupied retail space into a finished state. The lessor normally provides an allowance for you — or them — to perform this work.

Gross profit. Gross sales, less the cost of goods.

Inventory. As a noun, this means all of your store's stock that is in-tended for resale, or the value of same. As a verb, the act of count-ing and costing your business' stock.

Invoice. The bill for merchandise from a supplier that you use to pay. Not to be confused with statements, which are sent out monthly by some vendors, summarizing previous invoices and payments. Most vendors expect payment from the invoice.

Keystone. A retailing term for a 50 percent markup, which is equivalent to doubling the cost of goods to determine the selling price.

Layaway. Allowing customers to pay off a purchase over time, while you retain the goods. Normally requires payments over a relatively short period such as three months, with 25 percent down and three subsequent equal payments.

Lessee. You, as the renter of a space.

Lessor. The person or company from whom you rent.

Liability. Accounting term for debts your business owes, such as outstanding loans or accounts payable.

Market center. A regional wholesale center, where vendors and manufacturers display and sell their goods to you, the retailer. A sort of retail store for retailers, usually located in larger cities.

Markup. The percent of the selling price of an item that constitutes your gross profit. For example, an item that you sell for $1.00, for which you paid $0.75, would have a 25 percent markup. Remember that markup is figured on the selling price, not the cost.

Minimum. The smallest amount of goods a supplier will allow you to purchase, usually a dollar amount, but sometimes a quantity.

Net 30. Credit terms extended by a supplier, meaning you must pay the full amount within 30 days of shipment.

Net profit. Your gross profit, as defined above, less your expenses.

Payroll taxes. The taxes you must collect and pay based on a percentage of the gross wages of an employee. Always includes Social Security, Medicare, and federal unemployment tax, and usually includes state unemployment and other state, and sometimes local, taxes.

Profit and loss (P&L) statement. A financial report showing your sales, cost of goods, gross profits, and net profits for a given period.

Sales tax. A tax you must collect for and remit to a state or local government, usually a percent of gross sales. Only a handful of states do not levy a state sales tax.

Security deposit. A payment, usually one or more month's rent, normally demanded by lessors to protect them for any damages you may cause to their premises. It is refundable upon vacating the leased space.

Shopping mall. An enclosed, climate-controlled shopping area containing many varied stores, and typically anchored by two or more major department stores.

Single-entry bookkeeping. A simplified accounting system in which each expense or income item is entered only once. Does not provide the checks and balances and uniformity of a double-entry system.

Strip shopping center. A small group of stores joined together in a building, usually fronting a major thoroughfare. They usually have a common parking area, but each store has access to the street or common area.

Triple-net. A variable charge frequently added to your rent by lessors to cover taxes, insurance, and common-area maintenance.

Unemployment tax. A payroll tax levied by state and federal governments to finance payments to unemployed workers.

Withholding taxes. Amounts you are required to withhold from employees' wages for Social Security, Medicare, and income taxes, and deposit with the IRS. You must also withhold state income taxes and deposit these with your state's department of revenue. The taxes you withhold are in addition to the payroll taxes you must pay as an employer.

Useful
Publications

Magazines

Staying well-informed about local, state, and national business and buying trends can often mean the difference between success and failure. As a retail business owner, you will want to be informed of the newest, most innovative products for your store as well as keep an eye out for what is hot on a national level.

Local newspapers and state-specific magazines are valuable sources of local business news, but to stay in touch with nationwide business trends, consider subscribing to several national business publications. The magazines below represent only a sampling of the myriad publications that cover general business issues and specialty retailing and merchandise lines.

If your area of special interest is not covered by the list below, a complete listing of available trade and consumer publications, along with subscription rates, is available from:

Estrin & Diamond Publications
20832 Roscoe Boulevard
Canoga Park, CA 91306
(818) 700-6920

Meanwhile, the magazines below may be of interest. Call or write to inquire about subscription information or to request details about the publication's editorial content and special features.

Accessory Merchandising
400 Knightsbridge Parkway
Lincolnshire, IL 60069
(708) 634-2600

This publication provides information on new industry products and trends for owners, managers, and buyers in home furnishings, accessories, and department stores, with focuses on merchandising and specific decorative home accessory categories.

Collector's Mart Merchandiser
700 East State Street
Iola, WI 54990-0001
(800) 942-0673

This publication covers news in the field of limited edition collectible arts, with coverage of the U.S. and foreign buying markets. Trade show highlights and reviews of contemporary artists are featured, with focuses on prints, plates, dolls, cottages, ornaments, and figurines.

Country Business
707 Kautz Road
St. Charles, IL 60174
(708) 377-8000

This magazine provides business management expertise for retailers specializing in country merchandise. Not only is it a source for business advice, but also a wholesale buying resource. Articles cover successful marketing and merchandising techniques, industry trends, and new products.

Entrepreneur
Entrepreneur, Inc.
2392 Morse Avenue
Irvine, CA 92714
(714) 261-2325

This monthly publication features information on running a small business. Contains management tips, entrepreneurial success stories, franchise information, and news and reviews of the latest in office equipment.

Gift and Decorative Accessories
Subscription Service Center
51 Madison Avenue, 28th Floor
New York, NY 10010-1675
(800) 309-3332

This publication will be of interest to quality gift retailers of stationery, greeting cards, collectibles, china, glass, lamps, and accessories. Features include in-depth analyses of trends in gift merchandising and selling. Contains industry news, new product reviews, and trade literature. Includes previews of major markets.

Giftware News

P.O. Box 5398
Deptford, NJ 08096-0398
(609) 227-0798

This publication is written for gift, stationery, and department stores, as well as other retail outlets that sell giftware, stationery, tabletop and decorative accessories. New products, innovations in marketing and retailing techniques, and new trends in consumer buying comprise the regular features. Previews of major market shows are provided.

GSB: Gift & Stationery Business

One Penn Plaza
New York, NY 10119
(212) 714-1300

This magazine is written for the independent gift shop owner. Features include retailer profiles, new product information, analyses of industry trends, marketing and retailing techniques, display and store arrangement strategies, and entertaining articles related to the retail industry.

Home Accents Today

P.O. Box 2754
High Point, NC 27261-2754
(910) 605-0121

This publication, produced nine times a year, presents fashion news for the home accent and gift industries. Highlights include home accent and gift items, such as tabletop decor, lamps and shades, featuring the latest fashion styles and designs.

Home Lighting & Accessories

P.O. Box 2147
Clifton, NJ 07015
(201) 779-1600

This business magazine of the lighting industry, published by Doctorow Communications, highlights current happenings in the retail lighting industry, including current home furnishings, markets, and new products.

Inc.

38 Commercial Wharf
Boston, MA 02110
(800) 234-0999

This monthly publication emphasizes the critical contribution of the small firm to the American economy. *Inc.* provides managers of small to mid-sized privately held companies with information on management approaches in finance, marketing, and personnel, as well as profiles of leading growth companies and analyses of economic and policy trends affecting the contemporary small growth firm.

LDB Interior Textiles
2125 Center Avenue
Fort Lee, NJ 07204
(201) 592-7007

This publication monthly by E. W. Williams Publications highlights the latest trends in home fashions.

Small Business Opportunities
1115 Broadway
New York, NY 10010
(212) 807-7100

This is a monthly magazine that offers practical advice to entrepreneurs, plus regular features on numerous franchise opportunities throughout the country. It is a good source for researching franchise opportunities.

VM+SD – Visual Merchandising and Store Design
407 Gilbert Avenue
Cincinatti, OH 45202-2285
(513) 421-2050

This specialty magazine is directed towards professionals in the field of merchandise display and store interior design and planning.

Books from The Oasis Press

For more than a decade, the goal of every Oasis Press business book has been to provide practical, hands-on information in such a way that budding entrepreneurs or existing business owners could easily understand and apply the information to everyday business operations and use it to help ensure their success.

Book topics range from accounting to marketing and from insurance to business planning. Compiled below are several business books The Oasis Press feels are extremely valuable to supplement the many aspects of starting your own small retail business. To obtain one of the titles listed below, you can contact your local bookstore or The Oasis Press.

The Oasis Press/PSI Research
300 North Valley Drive
Grants Pass, OR 97526
(800) 228-2275

Business Owner's Guide to Accounting and Bookkeeping
This essential primer will help you interpret and prepare financial statements and organize your own set of books. $19.95.

The Buyer's Guide to Business Insurance
This book includes step-by-step guidance, ideas, and tips on how to improve your business insurance costs, coverage, and service from both agents and companies. This nontechnical reference guide shows you how to get the best property and casualty insurance coverage at the lowest price. $19.95.

Financing Your Small Business
This book features essential techniques to successfully identify, approach, attract, and manage sources of financing. It also shows you how to gain the full benefits of debt financing while minimizing its risks. A great book for beginning business owners. $19.95.

The Insider's Guide to Small Business Loans
This book informs the small business owner or upcoming entrepreneur what the key factors are for getting a small business loan, what to look for, and what to emphasize when putting together a business loan application. $19.95.

The Money Connection
This book is a listing of financing sources, such as venture capitalists, Small Business Investment Companies, and other public and private sources of funding for small businesses. Updated annually. $24.95.

Raising Capital: How to Write a Financing Proposal
This book shows you how to write a financing proposal to secure business loans, venture capital, or grants. $19.95.

Starting and Operating a Business in ... series
This helpful series of books covers all 50 states, plus the District of Columbia. Updated frequently, each book contains the latest state-specific and federal business information available. Learn about your state's taxes, laws, and the agencies created to help you start and operate your business more successfully! $24.95 for paperback or $29.95 for 3-ring binder.

Start Your Business: A Beginner's Guide
This book is for anyone who wants to start a business, who isn't sure about what it all entails, and who wants a brief overview of what is and can be involved in starting a business. It is designed for ease of use and to help create a plan of action for eight business topics. Compatible software is available. 2nd edition. $9.95.

Successful Business Plan: Secrets & Strategies
A start-to-finish guide to creating a successful business plan. Provides insider tips on writing a business plan and handy financials to make it easier to compile your information. Software and computer templates for several of the worksheets

found in the book are available in a variety of book/software combination packages. $21.95 for the paperback book. $49.95 for the business plan kit. $109.95 for the business plan kit and computer templates to use with your software. $125.95 for a standalone, executable software program and the business plan kit. Call for more information about the book and software packages.

Top Tax Saving Ideas for Today's Small Business

This layperson-friendly book takes the complex world of taxes and offers practical tax-saving solutions and strategies for the small business owner. The book covers topics such as home office expenses, tax write-offs for travel and entertainment, and how the latest tax laws will affect your future. $14.95.

Books from Other Publishers

In addition to The Oasis Press, several other book publishers and government agencies provide valuable titles that will help detail more of the aspects discussed in this book. Some of these titles, as well as their publishers, are listed below.

Circular E, Employer's Tax Guide
Internal Revenue Service (IRS)
Washington, DC
(800) 829-3676

An IRS publication that explains federal income tax withholding and Social Security tax requirements for employers. *Circular E* also contains up-to-date withholding tax tables so you can determine how much federal income tax and Social Security tax to withhold from employee paychecks.

Employer's Handbook
U.S. Immigration and Naturalization Service (INS)
Washington, DC
(800) 755-0777

A free publication to help employers deal with the department's procedures and forms. Call the number above or check your local phone listing for the INS office nearest you.

How to Comply with Federal Employee Laws
London Publishing
Washington, DC
(202) 296-7340

Updated in 1991, this easy-to-read book gives you the specifics you need to comply with federal employee laws. Good reference for the beginning business owner. Paperback edition costs $21.95 and includes shipping and handling.

The Legal Guide for Starting and Operating a Small Business
Nolo Press
Berkeley, CA
(510) 549-1976
(800) 992-6656

This guide is a comprehensive coverage of leases, with emphasis on avoiding legal problems. Its discussions cover short- and long-term leases, shopping center leases, additions and modifications, as well as advice on resolving disputes with landlords and getting legal advice. For more information, call the above number. $22.95.

Naming Your Business and Its Products and Services
The P. Gaines Publishing Company
Oak Park, IL
(800) 578-3853

A fun-to-read book on how to name your business. Good tips and advice for selecting a business name and a good source for learning how to research trade names, trademarks, and service marks effectively. $19.95.

Small-Time Operator
Bell Springs Publishing
Laytonville, CA
(707) 984-6746

Overall general start-up book written in everyday language that tackles the technical aspects of starting a business. It is also a workbook that includes bookkeeping instructions and a sample set of ledgers — all especially designed for the small business owner. $14.95.

Working Solo Sourcebook
Portico Press
New Paltz, NY
(914) 255-7165
FAX (914) 255-2116

This handy, easy-to-use reference book is your gateway to more than 1,200 essential business resources — each ready to guide you on the path to business success. With more than 40 subject headings, you have a large selection of business resources that are nicely organized and easy to locate. A very valuable reference for any new entrepreneur's desk. $14.95.

Small Business Administration Publications

The federal Small Business Administration (SBA) is one government agency that is genuinely helpful to small businesses. Among other services — such as providing free seminars and workshops, small business financing, and telephone hotlines — the SBA publishes numerous publications that you may find helpful.

→ *Business Plan for Retailers*, SBA #MP09 $2.00.

→ *Checklist for Going into Business*, SBA #MP12 $2.00.

→ *Inventory Management*, SBA #MP22 $2.00.

→ *Financing for Small Business*, SBA #FM14 $2.00.

→ *Financial Management for Growing Business*, SBA #EB07 $3.00.

→ *Management Issues for Growing Business*, SBA #EB03 $3.00.

→ *Pricing Your Products and Services Profitably*, SBA #FM13 $2.00.

→ *Record Keeping in a Small Business*, SBA #FM10 $2.00.

→ *Research Your Market*, SBA #MT08 $2.00.

→ *Understanding Cash Flow*, SBA #FM04 $2.00.

These publications are available from the SBA at the address listed below. You can also request a copy of the *Resource Directory for Small Business Management*, which lists these and other publications available from the SBA.

SBA Publications
P.O. Box 46521
Denver, CO 80201

Market, Gift, and Design Centers

The centers listed below are at fixed locations around the United States. In addition to gifts, most of the major centers also include, or are adjacent to, markets handling jewelry, apparel, furniture, home accessories, gourmet foods, kitchenware, and textiles.

Atlanta Market Center
Suite 2200
240 Peachtree Street NW
Atlanta, GA 30303
(404) 220-3000

The Bedford Center
59 Middlesex Turnpike
Bedford, MA 01730
(617) 275-2775

Charlotte Merchandise Mart
2500 East Independence Boulevard
Charlotte, NC 28205
(704) 333 7709

Chicago Merchandise Mart
200 World Trade Center
Chicago, IL 60654
(312) 527-4141

The Columbus Gift Mart
1999 West Belt Drive
Columbus, OH 43228
(614) 876-2719

Dallas Market Center
2100 Stemmons Freeway
Dallas, TX 75207
(214) 655-6100

Decoration & Design Building
979 Third Avenue
New York, NY 10022
(212) 759-8814

Denver Merchandise Mart
451 East 58th Avenue
Denver, CO 80216
(303) 292-6278

Eleven East Twenty-Sixth Street Building
11 East 26th Street
New York, NY 10010
(212) 683-5262

Giftcenter & Jewelry Mart
888 Brannan Street
San Francisco, CA 94103
(415) 861-7733

Indianapolis Gift Mart
4475 Allisonville Road
Indianapolis, IN 46205
(317) 546-0719

International Home Furnishings Center
210 East Commerce Street
High Point, NC 27260
(910) 888-6688

225 – The International Showcase
225 5th Avenue
New York, NY 10010
(212) 684-3200

Kansas City Merchandise Mart
6800 West 115th Street
Overland Park, KS 66211
(913) 491-6688

The L.A. Mart
1933 South Broadway
Los Angeles, CA 90007
(213) 749-7911

The Market Center
230 5th Avenue
New York, NY 10001
(212) 372-2377

Miami Merchandise Mart
777 NW 72nd Avenue
Miami, FL 33136
(305) 261-2900

Michigan Association of Gift Salesmen
133 West Main Street
Northville, MI 48167
(313) 348-7890

Minneapolis Gift Mart
10301 Bren Road West
Minnetonka, MN 55343
(612) 932-7200

New York Merchandise Mart
41 Madison Avenue
New York, NY 10010
(212) 686-1203

Philadelphia Home Furnishings Market
P.O. Box 250
Carlisle, PA 17013
(717) 243-9225

Pittsburg Expo Mart
105 Mall Boulevard
Monroeville, PA 15146
(412) 856-8100

Exhibition Companies and Trade Associations

Trade associations represent specific segments of the retailing industry and can provide information about suppliers of specific goods. Exhibition management companies manage and stage periodic wholesale shows around the United States. These shows cover a broad spectrum of geography and merchandise and are usually held during the same period each year. They do not always have a permanent facility, but use local exhibition halls, auditoriums, and even hotel convention facilities.

The Heritage Wholesale Markets, for example, have winter and summer shows around Valley Forge, Pennsylvania, using several hotels and local exhibition halls around Philadelphia. Many of the companies sponsor several shows at different times and places. You can write or call the following management companies for a listing of types and locations of currently planned events.

AMC Trade Shows, Ltd.
 A Portman Co.
888 South Figuroa Street, Suite 600
Los Angeles, CA 90017
(213) 747-3488

Americana Sampler
P.O. Box 16009
Nashville, TN 37216
(615) 227-2080

American Association of Exporters and Importers, Inc.
11 West 42nd Street, 30th Floor
New York, NY 10036
(212) 944-2230

American Craft Council
72 Spring Street
New York, NY 10012
(212) 274-0630

American Gift & Art Shows
100 Bickford Street
Rochester, NY 14806
(716) 254-2580

American Pewter Guild, Ltd.
11940 Old Buckingham Road
Midlothian, VA 23113
(804) 379-3282

Art Buyers Caravan Trade Show
330 North 4th Street
Saint Louis, MO 63102
(314) 421-5445

Association of Crafts & Creative Individuals
1100-H Brandywine Boulevard
P.O. Box 2188
Zanesville, OH 43702
(614) 452-4541

Bass Shows, Inc.
P.O. Box 1705
Brockton, MA 02403
(508) 583-8351

Beckman's Gift Show Industry Productions of America, Inc.
875 North Gower
Los Angeles, CA 90038
(213) 962-5424

Blenheim Group
Fort Lee Executive Park
Fort Lee, NJ 07024
(800) 829-3976

Charlotte Gift, Jewelry, & Housewares Show
800 Briarcreek Road, Suite BB503
Charlotte, NC 28205
(704) 377-5881

Chicago Giftware Association
1501 Merchandise Mart
Chicago, IL 60654
(312) 321-0563

The Color Marketing Group
5904 Richmond Highway, #408
Alexandria, VA 22303
(703) 329-8500

Copper Development Association
260 Madison Avenue, 16th Floor
New York, NY 10016
(212) 251-7200

DMC Expositions
1601 Stemmons Freeway, Suite F
Dallas, TX 75207
(214) 744-3131

Douglas Trade Shows
P.O. Box 1087
Kaneohe, HI 96744
(808) 254-1773

Epic Enterprises
8989 Rio San Diego Drive, Suite 160
San Diego, CA 92108
(619) 294-2999

The Fragrance Foundation
145 East 32nd Street
New York, NY 10016
(212) 725-2755

George Little Management
10 Bank Street, Suite 1200
White Plains, NY 10606
(914) 421-3200

Gift Association of America, Inc.
612 West Broad Street
Bethlehem, PA 18018-5221
(610) 861-9445

Gift Retailers, Manufacturers, & Representatives Association
1100-H Brandywine Boulevard
P.O. Box 2188
Zanesville, OH 43702-2188
(614) 452-4541

Greeting Card Association
1200 G Street NW, Suite 760
Washington, DC 20005
(202) 393-1778

Heritage Wholesale Market
P.O. Box 389
Carlisle, PA 17013
(717) 249-9404

Hobby Industries of America
319 East 54th Street
P.O. Box 348
Elmwood Park, NJ 07407
(201) 794-1133

Independent Expositions
221 King Manor Drive
King of Prussia, PA 19406
(610) 272-4025

International Mass Retailer Association
1700 North Moor Street, #2250
Arlington, VA 22209
(703) 841-2300

Jewelers of America, Inc.
1185 6th Avenue, 30th Floor
New York, NY 10036
(212) 768-8777

Juvenile Products Manufacturers Association
236 Route 38 West
Moorestown, NJ 08057
(604) 231-8500

Karel Expositions
P.O. Box 222008
Hollywood Beach, FL 33022
(305) 454-7777

Kentucky Craft Marketing Program
39 Fountain Place
Frankfort, KY 40601
(502) 564-8076

Luggage & Leather Goods Manufacturers of America, Inc.
350 5th Avenue, Suite 2624
New York, NY 10118
(212) 695-2340

Market Square Wholesale
313 South Hanover Street
Carlisle, PA 17013
(717) 245-9031

Miller Freeman Trade Shows
110 Plaza
New York, NY 10119
(212) 714-1300

National Association for the Specialty Food Trade, Inc.
8 West 40th Street, 4th Floor
New York, NY 10018-3901
(212) 921-1690

National Association of Balloon Artists
1205 West Forsyth Street
Jacksonville, FL 32204
(904) 354-7271

National Association of Bridal Consultants
200 Chestnutland Road
New Milford, CT 06776
(203) 355-0464

National Association of Limited Edition Dealers
5235 Monticello Avenue
Dallas, TX 75206
(800) 446-2533

National Bridal Service
3122 West Cary Street
Richmond, VA 23221
(804) 355-6945

National Candle Association
1200 G Street NW, Suite 760
Washington, DC 20005
(202) 393-1780

National Housewares Association
6400 Shafer Court, Suite 650
Rosemont, IL 60018
(708) 292-4200

National Luggage Dealers Association
245 Fifth Avenue, # 601
New York, NY 10016
(212) 684-1610

National Retail Federation
325 7th Street NW, # 1000
Washington, DC 20004
(202) 783-7971

National Tabletop Association
355 Lexington Avenue, 17th Floor
New York, NY 10017
(212) 661-4261

New England Gift Show Association
P.O. Box 1705
Brockton, MA 02403
(508) 583-8351

New York Tabletop & Accessories Show
1011 Clifton Avenue
Clifton, NJ 07015
(201) 779-1600

North Lakes Gift Shows, Inc.
208 Mill Road
Manitowoc, WI 54220
(414) 682-6225

O.A.S.I.S. Gift Show
1130 East Missouri Street, # 750
Phoenix, AZ 85014
(602) 230-1237

Photo Marketing Association International
3000 Picture Place
Jackson, MI 49201
(517) 788-8100

Progressive Exhibitors, Inc. Salt Lake Gift Show
320 East, 200 South
Salt Lake City, UT 84111
(801) 973-7800

Rome Enterprises
4208 Rivanna Drive
Louisville, KY 40299-3473
(502) 267-7663

The Rosen Group
Mill Center
3000 Chestnut Avenue, Suite 300
Baltimore, MD 21211
(410) 889-2933

Southern Shows, Inc.
810 Baxter Street
P.O. Box 36859
Charlotte, NC 28236
(704) 376-6594

Toy Manufacturers of America, Inc.
200 Fifth Avenue, Room 740
New York, NY 10010
(212) 675-1141

Urban Expositions
P.O. Box 672524
Marietta, GA 30067
(404) 952-6444

Western Exhibitors, Inc.
2181 Greenwich Street
San Francisco, CA 94123
(415) 346-6666

Index

Establish A Framework
For Excellence With The
Successful Business Library

Fastbreaking changes in technology and the global marketplace continue to create unprecedented opportunities for businesses through the '90s. With these opportunities, however, will also come many new challenges. Today, more than ever, businesses, especially small businesses, need to excel in all areas of operation to complete and succeed in an ever-changing world.

The Successful Business Library takes you through the '90s and beyond, helping you solve the day-to-day problems you face now, and prepares you for the unexpected problems you may be facing next. You receive up-to-date and practical business solutions, which are easy to use and easy to understand. No jargon or theories, just solid, nuts-and-bolts information.

Whether you are an entrepreneur going into business for the first time or an experienced consultant trying to keep up with the latest rules and regulations, The Successful Business Library provides you with the step-by-step guidance, and action-oriented plans you need to succeed in today's world. As an added benefit, PSI Research / The Oasis Press® unconditionally guarantees your satisfaction with the purchase of any book or software program in our catalog.

Your success is our success...

At PSI Research and The Oasis Press, we take pride in helping you and 2 million other businesses grow. It's the same pride we take in watching our own business grow from two people working out of a garage in 1975 to more than 50 employees now in our award-winning building in scenic southern Oregon.

 After all, your business is our business.

Call Toll Free To Receive A Free Catalog Or To Place An Order
1 - 8 0 0 - 2 2 8 - 2 2 7 5
All Major Credit Cards Accepted

PSI Research, 300 North Valley Drive, Grants Pass, OR 97526
(800) 228-2275 (541) 479-9464 FAX (541) 476-1479

Books that save you time and money...

Straightforward advice on shopping for insurance, understanding types of coverage, comparing proposals and premium rates. Worksheets help identify and weigh the risks a particular business is likely to face, then helps determine if any of those might be safely self-insured or eliminated. Request for proposal forms help businesses avoid over-paying for protection.

Buyer's Guide to Business Insurance   **Pages: 280**
Paperback : $19.95   **ISBN: 1-55571-162-6**
Binder Edition: $39.95   **ISBN: 1-55571-310-6**

Essential techniques to successfully identify, approach, attract, and manage sources of financing. Shows how to gain the full benefits of debt financing while minimizing its risks. Outlines all types of financing and carefully walks you through the process, from evaluating short-term credit options, through negotiating a long-term loan, to deciding whether to go public.

Financing Your Small Business   **Pages: 214**
Paperback: $19.95   **ISBN: 1-55571-160-X**

Essential for the small business operator in search of capital, this helpful, hands-on guide simplifies the loan application process. *The Insider's Guide to Small Business Loans* is an easy-to-follow roadmap designed to help you cut through the red tape and show you how to prepare a successful loan application. Packed with helpful resources, such as SBIC directories, SBA offices, microloan lenders, and a complete nationwide listing of certified and preferred lenders — plus more than a dozen invaluable worksheets and forms.

The Insider's Guide to Small Business Loans   **Pages: 260**
Paperback: $19.95   **ISBN: 1-55571-373-4**
Binder Edition: $29.95   **ISBN: 1-55571-378-5**

An extensive summary of every imaginable tax break that is still available in today's "reform" tax environment. Deals with the various entities that the owner/manager may choose to operate a business. Identifies a wide assortment of tax deduction, fringe benefits, and tax deferrals. Includes a simplified checklist of recent tax law changes with an emphasis on tax breaks.

Top Tax Saving Ideas for Today's Small Business   **Pages: 320**
Paperback: $15.95   **ISBN: 1-55571-379-3**

Call toll free to order 1-800-228-2275   FAX 541-476-1479

PSI Research   300 North Valley Drive, Grants Pass, OR 97526

Books that save you time and money...

Makes understanding the economics of your business simple. Explains the basic accounting principles that relate to any business. Step-by-step instructions for generating accounting statements and interpreting them, spotting errors, and recognizing warning signs. Discusses how creditors view financial statements.

Business Owners' Guide to Accounting and Bookkeeping   **Pages: 146**
Paperback: $19.95   **ISBN: 1-55571-385-1**

Written for the business owner or manager who is not a personnel specialist. Explains what you must know to make your hiring decisions pay off for everyone. Learn more about the Americans With Disabilities Act (ADA), Medical and Family Leave, and more.

People Investment   **Pages: 210**
Paperback: $19.95   **ISBN: 1-55571-161-8**
Binder Edition: $39.95   **ISBN: 1-55571-187-1**

Now you can find out what venture capitalists and bankers really want to see before they will fund a company. This book gives you their personal tips and insights. The Abrams Method of Flow-Through Financials breaks down the chore into easy-to-manage steps, so you can end up with a fundable proposal.

Successful Business Plan: Secrets & Strategies   **Pages: 340**
Paperback: $24.95   **ISBN: 1-55571-194-4**
Binder Edition: $49.95   **ISBN: 1-55571-197-9**

Our best seller for 13 years – still your best source of practical business information. Find out what new laws affect your business. Now there's an edition for every state in the U.S., plus the District of Columbia.

Starting & Operating a Business in ... series
Paperback: $24.95
Binder Workbook Edition: $29.95

Specify which state you want.

Call toll free to order 1-800-228-2275   FAX 541-476-1479

PSI Research   300 North Valley Drive, Grants Pass, OR 97526

REDE3/96

...ctly from The Oasis Press

To order or for a complete catalog call toll free 1-800-228-2275

Mail or Fax to:
PSI Research / The Oasis Press
300 North Valley Drive
Grants Pass, OR 97526 USA

Inquiries and International Orders (541) 479-9464
FAX (541) 476-1479

Title	Binder	Paperback	Quantity	Cost
Buyer's Guide to Business Insurance	☐ $39.95	☐ $19.95		
Financing Your Small Business		☐ $19.95		
Insider's Guide to Small Business Loans	☐ $29.95	☐ $19.95		
Top Tax Saving Ideas for Today's Small Business		☐ $15.95		
Business Owner's Guide to Accounting & Bookkeeping		☐ $19.95		
People Investment	☐ $19.95	☐ $39.95		
Successful Business Plan: Secrets & Strategies	☐ $49.95	☐ $24.95		
Starting & Operating a Business in... book	☐ $29.95	☐ $24.95		

PLEASE SPECIFY WHICH STATE(S) YOU WANT: _____

_____

_____

If your purchase is:	Shipping within the USA:
$0 - $25	$5.00
$25.01 - $50	$6.00
$50.01 - $100	$7.00
$100.01 - $175	$9.00
$175.01 - $250	$13.00
$250.01 - $500	$18.00
$500.01 +	4% of total merchandise

SUBTOTAL

SHIPPING

TOTAL ORDER

International or Canadian orders, please call for a quote on shipping costs.

SOLD TO: *Please give street address.*

Name: _____

Title: _____

Company: _____

Street Address: _____

City/State/Zip: _____

Daytime Phone: _____

PAYMENT INFORMATION: *Rush service is available. Call for details.*

CHECK enclosed payable to PSI Research   CHARGE VISA MASTERCARD AMEX DISCOVER

Card Number: _____   Expires: _____

Signature: _____   Name on Card: _____